Presented to:

_____

From:

_____

Date:

_____

Make Your Day Count
Devotional
for Mothers

Presented by

Lindsay Roberts and Friends

Harrison House
Tulsa, Oklahoma

Make Your Day Count Devotional for Mothers
ISBN 1-57794-662-6
Copyright © 2004 by Lindsay Roberts
Oral Roberts Ministries
Tulsa, Oklahoma 74171-0001

Published by Harrison House, Inc.
P.O. Box 35035
Tulsa, Oklahoma 74153

Manuscript compiled and edited by Betsy Williams of Williams Services, Inc., Tulsa, Oklahoma;
www.williams.services.inc@cox.net.

Contents

Introduction

Chances are, you're like me—you lead a busy life with many demanding responsibilities. Not only is it your job to keep your home flowing smoothly, you are a full-time taxi driver, cheerleader, confidante, nurse, and life instructor. Whether you are a work-at-home mom or a mom who has a career outside the home, your days are no doubt jam-packed and your to-do list never-ending. But do you and your children always get off to a good start each morning?

What we do first thing in the morning sets the tone for the rest of the day. The purpose of this book is to give you a bite-sized bit of godly wisdom shared by some of the most outstanding women in the body of Christ today. Then we've included an action step, something practical you can do each day to apply what you've learned.

Sprinkled throughout you will find some helpful hints and quick-and-easy, mouth-watering recipes I hope your family will enjoy. My goal, and that of the other contributors, is to help you start each day on the right track and *make your day count!*

Blessings,
Lindsay

Someone to Watch Over You

Lindsay Roberts

Lead me in thy truth, and teach me: for thou art the
God of my salvation; on thee do I wait all the day.
—Psalm 25:5 KJV

We all need someone to watch over us and lead us in the right direction from time to time. For me, one of those people has always been my mother.

I was only twelve years old when my father died of cancer. My mother raised my brother, my sister, and me by herself in the turbulent sixties. I watched her not just talk about God's Word, but live its truths every day. And because she did, we constantly saw miracles in our household and came to know that God is real.

Mother walked around talking to God as though He was right in the room. My friends would ask, "Who's she talking to?"

I'd answer, "She's talking to the Lord," as if it was the most natural thing in the world.

When my brother, sister, or I asked for permission to do things, she always said, "I'll pray about it." That meant, "Not until God says it's okay." We had to go through Mom and God to get permission to do anything! But that's how God became real to us, and today we're all living for Him.

Being a mom isn't always easy, but the good news is, you are never alone. Your heavenly Father is always there, always watching over you, always helping you to be the best mom you can be. Let Him help you today.[1]

make **your** day count

As your children express needs to you today, take those very moments to pray with them, reminding them that when they pray according to God's promises, He always answers.

Teach Them While They're Young

Evelyn Roberts

Jesus said, "Let the little children come to me, and don't prevent them. For of such is the Kingdom of Heaven." And he put his hands on their heads and blessed them.
—Matthew 19:14–15 TLB

To be entrusted with a precious child is one of life's sweetest joys, greatest privileges, and heaviest responsibilities. Our children can receive no greater heritage from us than to be taught to read the Word, to pray, and to look to Jesus as the One who knows and understands each problem and has a solution. It's never too early to start teaching your children that God loves them completely and unconditionally and that they need never be afraid to come to Him.

From the time our children were able to talk, Oral took them on his knee, told them Bible stories, and had them learn to recite Scripture verses. They learned that the promises of God are for them, just as they were for people in the Bible.

We tried to build a sense of God's goodness into our children's daily lives. We taught them that God is a good God, that everybody is somebody in God's eyes, and that He is concerned about every part of our lives. No need is too big or too small.

Children pick up what we say and do even when we don't realize they are listening and observing us. I recommend that parents know the Lord for themselves and then saturate their children with the Word of God.[2]

make **your** day count

Not only are your children special to you, but they are even more important to God. Today, think of a specific way in which God has shown that He considers each of them to be a somebody in His eyes. Then share your thoughts with them.

A Mother's Love

Patricia Salem

Train a child in the way he should go,
and when he is old he will not turn from it.
—Proverbs 22:6

I believe that being a mother is God's highest calling for a woman because it's a calling to nurture the next generation. And I believe the greatest gift a mother can give her children is love, especially God's love. Sometimes that love has to be tough. It sets guidelines, showing our children which way they should go according to God's Word and correcting them when necessary.

Prayer is one of the secrets to a mother's success. As a widow at age thirty-eight, I made God my husband (according to Isa. 54:5), consulting Him on everything. I'd say, "Lord, I'm not leaving here until You tell me how to handle this situation," and He was always there. He wants to give us the answers we need, because He loves our children even more than we do!

It's also important for mothers to speak loving words of faith over their children. From the moment I knew I was pregnant, I said to my children in the womb, "You will serve the Lord every day of your life," and all of them have.

Children may not look like they are responding to your love and prayers, but no matter what they have done or where they are today, never give up. Keep loving them and praying for them, because God loves your family, and He is faithful![3]

make **your** day count

It is often difficult for children to understand how discipline and training reflect your love for them. As opportunities arise today to love them in these ways, take a moment to remind your children that you believe in them. Then explain how your specific actions reflect your great love.

time **saving** tips

A Stress-Free Before-School Routine[4]

Anyone who has ever had to get children ready for school each morning knows how stressful it can be—not a good way to start the day! Try some of these tips that will promote peace and order. They will help both you and your children get off on the right foot each morning, so you can make your day count!

 Pack lunches the night before and refrigerate.

 Look over any school papers, notes from teachers, and assignment guides the night before.

 Make sure backpacks are packed and ready to go the night before.

 Create a homework center, stocked with extra crayons and supplies needed to complete homework. Make sure it's not near a TV.

 Lay out clothes the night before.

 Create a special hamper in the laundry room for uniforms and other rush items.

 Each evening have a thirty-minute family cleanup time to put everything back into place.

easy **recipes**

Caramel Corn[5]

Patricia Salem

4 to 6 quarts popped popcorn
2 cups brown sugar
1 cup butter
1 cup light corn syrup
$\frac{1}{2}$ tsp. cream of tartar
$\frac{1}{2}$ tsp. baking soda

Pop the corn according to package directions and set aside in a large bowl.

In a heavy saucepan, add sugar, butter, and corn syrup and bring to a boil.

Cook 5 minutes on medium heat, stirring constantly. (Make sure it keeps boiling.)

Remove from heat. Add cream of tartar and baking soda. Mix well with popped corn.

Put on cookie sheet and bake at 200° for 1 hour.

This is a treat for my grandchildren. It makes a large batch, but we usually don't store it. You can, however, put it in a plastic container for several days. It does store well.

Protection in Dangerous Times

Kellie Copeland Kutz

*The LORD gives wisdom, and from his mouth come
knowledge and understanding. He holds victory in
store for the upright, he is a shield to those whose
walk is blameless, for he guards the course of the just
and protects the way of his faithful ones.*
—Proverbs 2:6–8

As a mother, you know only too well that overriding
desire to protect your children from harm. You deal with it
every time you send your children out the door to school or
watch your teenagers drive off with their friends. What can
you do as a mother to ensure that your children are protected
every moment of the day?

I began seeking the Lord about this after my cousin Nikki
was killed in a car accident involving a drunk driver. Nikki
was Miss "On Fire for God," one of the most phenomenal
people I have ever known. Nikki's death was a huge wake-up
call for me. I prayed, "Lord, I want You to show me how we
let this happen. What do we need to do to make sure it never
happens again?"

God immediately began to answer that prayer. He taught
me four primary things we must do to ensure the protection
of those we love: plead the blood of Jesus, take advantage of
angelic protection, listen to our spirits, and discipline our

children. Developing rock-solid confidence in these principles is the goal you should be aiming for as a believer, and as
you do, your faith will grow and you can know that your
children—as well as all whom you love—are safe.[6]

make **your** day count

Gather your children around you today. Plead the blood of
Jesus over them, and send forth their angels to protect them.
Ask God to teach you to hear His voice, to make you aware of danger.
Remind your children as you discipline them that the Bible promises
long life to those who will honor and obey their parents.*

---

* See Ephesians 6:1-2.

Losing Weight One Step at a Time

Marty Copeland

Precept must be upon precept, precept upon precept; line
upon line, line upon line; here a little, and there a little.
—Isaiah 28:10 KJV

It should be no surprise that when believers have tried to win the battle of the bulge through ordinary human strength, they've failed. I know because I have been there. But you can get there from here.

First, get to know Jesus. The spiritual things have to come first because you are a spirit. You live in a body. If you want your spirit to dominate your body, you have to feed your spirit.

Second, we've known ordinary human wisdom. For example, eat fewer calories than you burn, and you will lose weight. That's a fact, but there's no power in knowing that. When temptation to overeat comes, we must immediately draw strength from God's Word to cast those thoughts down.

Third, concentrate on the "do's" and not on the "don'ts." While drinking six to eight glasses of water, eating two to three fruits and three to seven servings of vegetables a day may be our ultimate goal, we don't start there. Begin drinking four or five glasses of water each day and eating at least two pieces of fruit and two vegetables each day. If you will take one step of faith at a time to do something that you are not already doing, step by step you will eventually meet your goal.[7]

make **your** day count

With your ultimate goal in mind, what is one thing you could
do today that would be a single step toward that goal?
Step out and do that one thing today.

Warming the Nest

Marilyn Hickey

She speaks with wisdom,
and faithful instruction is on her tongue.
She watches over the affairs of her household.
—Proverbs 31:26–27

One of the best things that parents can do for their children is to develop the right atmosphere in the home, or what I call "warm the nest." Frequently we find that even though we are Christians and have a good relationship with the Lord, our home situation is not a warm one.

We must look to what God's Word says about our situation rather than what we see happening around us. Frequently, when everything is going wrong in our family relationships, we tend to look for someone to blame. "What's happening in my home?" we ask. "It's my wife! If she weren't such a nag, we'd have good family relationships." Or, "It's my husband! If he weren't such a bum, we'd have a marvelous home." Or, "It's that rebellious teenager of ours! If it weren't for him, we'd have a peaceful home!"

We always like to put the cause of disharmony in the family on some other member in the family, but the Bible teaches us that as wives and mothers, we are to set the atmosphere in the home. One way we can do that is by finding out what God says about the home in His Word. We can pray those promises over our homes, and God will bring them to pass.

You are the one to "warm your nest"—not your mate and not your children. Don't say, "Well, it's because of our circumstances." God will help you overcome negative circumstances![8]

make **your** day count

Think of a specific thing you can do today to "warm your nest."
Then receive God's strength through meditating on His Word.
Pray for God's grace, peace, love, and joy to fill your home.

Shaping Your Children's Future

Taffi L. Dollar

Write the vision and make it plain on tablets,
that he may run who reads it. For the vision
is yet for an appointed time.
—Habakkuk 2:2–3 NKJV

As a mother, you are responsible for nurturing, training, and imparting vision to your children. Proverbs 29:18 KJV states, "Where there is no vision, the people perish." Without a vision, your children are more likely to become undisciplined and uncommitted to fulfilling the will of God for their lives. This is why it is important that you begin imparting vision to them as early as possible, so they will want to discover and actively participate in God's divine plan.

How can you determine where God is leading your children? Examine their natural talents and interests. Determine whether they excel in sports, science, the arts, or church-related activities. Pay attention to their strengths and enroll them in programs that will assist them in developing their talents.

It is also important to help your children set short- and long-term goals. A short-term goal in team sports, for example, would be for your child to become the best player on his or her team. A long-term goal would involve discovering your child's career objectives and deciding on the best avenues for achieving them.

Perhaps the most important element of parenting is to instill in your children the image of God and His righteousness, always letting love guide your actions. It will position them to receive the divine inheritance that is theirs as heirs of salvation through Christ![9]

make **your** day count

Take a few moments today to write down the talents and strengths of each of your children. Then, set aside a time with each of them, perhaps one child per day, and share your observations. Discuss ways that each strength could relate to their future, and pray with them, asking God to reveal His perfect will for their lives.

time **saving** tips

Marriage Rejuvenators

Betsy Williams

We take our cars in for regular maintenance; we go to the dentist to prevent cavities; we go the family physician for regular checkups. Marriages need occasional tune-ups too. Try some of these quick tips to jumpstart a marriage that may be stuck in a rut or reenergize an already fulfilling relationship.

 Send your spouse off to work with a hug and a kiss tomorrow morning. Greet him with the same when he returns. (Be sure to brush your teeth!)

 Send a funny card to your husband at his place of employment.

 Go on a walk around your neighborhood or through the mall and hold hands, interlocking your fingers.

 Eat dinner across the table from one another and look your hubby in the eye as he tells you about his day. Really listen.

 E-mail your husband just to say you care.

Take your husband's hands in yours and pray with him about a concern he has.

Take out one of those hot-looking pieces of lingerie and wear it!

Easy Fruit Cobbler

Betsy Williams

1 stick butter or margarine
1 cup sugar
1 cup flour
1 cup milk
1 Tbsp. baking powder
1 can sliced or cut up fruit
(Peaches, blueberries, blackberries, or cherries are good choices)

Melt butter in a 1 ½-qt. baking dish.

Mix dry ingredients and pour over butter. Do not stir.

Remove 2 Tbsp. of juice from canned fruit.

Pour milk then fruit with remaining juice over flour mixture. Do not stir.

Cook uncovered at 375° for at least 35 minutes.

Great with vanilla ice cream served on top!

My Greatest Harvest

Lindsay Roberts

They that sow in tears shall reap in joy.
—Psalm 126:5 KJV

Is there an area of your life that seems barren? I know what that feels like. At the age of 18, I was told that I'd never have a child. After Richard and I were married, I had two miscarriages and a tumor the size of a grapefruit on my only functioning ovary. After God miraculously removed that tumor and I became pregnant, I endured the death of our firstborn child, Richard Oral, just thirty-six hours after his birth. All total, there were ten long years of heartbreak and failure.

In the midst of my hopelessness, God began to minister to my heart to give baby showers. Learning to plant a seed of my heart's desire during a time of famine was one of the hardest things I've ever done. But *if you don't plant seed, you will not have a harvest.* One time I had a miscarriage just three days before I gave a baby shower!

I'd serve the cake, give presents, and be so nice. Then after everyone went home, I'd go upstairs and cry until I thought my insides would fall out. But I knew that if I didn't plant seed in the midst of my famine, I would always live in famine.

It was hard, but planting those baby showers was worth it. Today, Richard and I have three beautiful daughters, and I

can tell you from experience that those who sow in tears *shall*
reap in joy! [10]

make **your** day count

Is there an area in your life that is barren? Plant a seed today
of the very thing you are believing God to provide.
Receive His comfort and strength to encourage you.

Intimacy in Marriage Starts with Friendship

Brenda Timberlake-White

[Jesus said], "Greater love has no one than this, that he lay down his life for his friends."
—John 15:13

Most couples think they are friends before they marry, but then somehow "lose" their friendship after the wedding. But God's plan is that the person you are married to should be the best and most intimate friend you have!

If your marriage lacks intimacy, you may need to backtrack. A house must be built upon a strong foundation that has had time to settle in order for it to be sturdy. Likewise, intimacy doesn't happen overnight. Intimacy is not love at first sight. You can have the "hots" for someone you see for the first time, but you cannot love that person because you do not know him or her. Intimacy has to be developed over many hours of conversing; it involves knowing the heart of the person.

Intimacy in marriage is partly sexual, but it involves much more. It is a close relationship between two people who deeply love and appreciate one another, regardless of shortcomings and failures. It loves like Jesus loves, laying its life down for its friend, loving without limit. It is totally

accepting and forgiving. An intimate friend loves out of com-
mitment, not on condition.

Developing intimacy in marriage takes hard work, but
there's nothing that can compare to being married to your
best friend. It's a little bit of heaven, right here on earth—
well worth the investment.[11]

make **your** day count

If you are married, make a date with your spouse to just sit and talk. Treat your
spouse as you would any friend whom you are trying to get to know better.
Ask questions and show genuine interest as your spouse answers.

Fearfully and Wonderfully Made

Pat Harrison

I praise you because I am fearfully and wonderfully made;
your works are wonderful, I know that full well.

—Psalm 139:14

You are a woman by birth—God does not make mistakes. Rejoice that He skillfully crafted you, and understand that it is okay to be the unique individual He has created you to be.

I know about this from personal experience. I had a difficult time learning that it was all right to be me. When I was younger, I was shy, introverted, and easily intimidated. I set no boundaries with others, so people felt free to walk all over me.

I could not function the way I needed to as long as fear and torment ruled my life. I had to find out that it was okay to be who I was and to set boundaries. I had to learn what I liked and didn't like and that I wanted things to be according to God's Word. I had to allow the Word of God and the Holy Spirit to change me.

Instead of trying to please people, focus on pleasing God first. Allow Him to work in you and change you into that person He intended. He has specifically called *you* to be and to do certain things, but He will never ask you to be someone you cannot be.

Discover the real you. Then be the best you that you can be.[12]

make **your** day count

Ask God to reveal the real you and to give you the strength you need to shine. Perhaps writing in a journal would be a good way to let your thoughts flow freely. There never has been and never will be another you. Be who God made you to be.

time **saving** tips

Alternative Sweeteners

To promote good health, try some of the alternative sweet-
eners to replace sugar: honey, molasses, Sucranat, and the
herb stevia. All of these are available at health-food stores.

Sucranat is natural, unrefined cane sugar, rich in
minerals and vitamins. It can be substituted cup for
cup to replace white or brown sugar. It works especially well in baked goods such as oatmeal cookies,
carrot cake, banana nut bread, and bran muffins.[13]

Stevia comes in both liquid and powdered form. It is
an excellent substitute for sugar and artificial sweet-
eners because it is a natural herb. Although it is
200–300 times sweeter than sugar, it contains no
calories or carbohydrates and it does not trigger a
rise in blood sugar. It works especially well in drinks
such as coffee and both hot and iced tea.[14]

Be sure to check with your doctor before making any
changes in your diet.

Southern Pecan Pie[15]

Pat Harrison

1 cup sugar

3 eggs

2 Tbsp. flour

¾ cup dark corn syrup

2 Tbsp. butter

1 tsp. vanilla

1½ cups of large pecan pieces

1 unbaked pie shell

Mix all together and pour into unbaked pie shell.

Bake at 275° to 300° for 1 hour.

Preventative Praying

Marilyn Hickey

[Jesus said], "If you believe, you will receive whatever you ask for in prayer."
—Matthew 21:22

Luke 8:11 says that the Word of God is a seed. It is never bad seed. Rather, it is incorruptible; it cannot decay. It has to come up, but it doesn't always come up at the time we are expecting it. That is especially true if you plant a seed today and expect it to produce tomorrow.

I have noticed that at times I have prayed over an immediate need, but I did not see the answer until three or four months later. The Lord began to deal with me about this. He said, *It takes time for seed to come up. You don't expect carrots to come up the day after you plant them, do you? Pray now for tomorrow's needs.*

I'm learning to plan *now* for what my children will need in the future, perhaps ten years from now. I believe there is much planting that we can do by praying for our children, our families, and the needs that we will have in the future. That is what I call "preventative praying." Too many times when we have a big emergency, we enter into "curative praying," which takes much more effort and can be a very frustrating battle. The important thing is to pray and believe

God's promises *now* for the needs of the future; then when
the time comes, you can reap the results.[16]

make **your** day count

Think of a couple of important issues that your children will have to deal
with in the future, such as their choice of career, their marriage partner,
their relationship with God. Plant seed in prayer today, so your
children will reap God's blessing in those areas tomorrow.

A Fruitful Time of Exercise

Marty Copeland

Bodily exercise profits a little, but godliness
is profitable for all things.
—1 Timothy 4:8 NKJV

I work out three to five times per week, and honestly, I rarely want to; but I have trained myself to do it. I make a deal with myself every time and say, "Marty, get dressed and just get on the treadmill." That doesn't seem too difficult.

I rarely intend to run two or three miles. I always set my goal at one mile. But once I've completed one mile, I often say, "I'm going to go another half mile today." Invariably, I run at least two miles.

You know what really helps me? During my exercise time, I say a prayer that is based on several Scriptures*: "Father God, I present my body to You as a living sacrifice. I offer this time of exercise to You as a time of worship—to glorify You in my body. I purpose in my heart to sow seeds of self-control, endurance, and faithfulness, and I believe I receive a one-hundredfold return. I earnestly expect to become more and more like Jesus, therefore I press on toward that goal, for the prize of my high calling. I decree that with every step I take, I am increasing in health, strength, and discipline. Thank You for anointing me to succeed as I prove Your good and perfect will in my life. In Jesus' name, amen."[17]

make **your** day count

Set a small, achievable fitness goal today and go about doing it.
It could be as simple as choosing to climb stairs wherever
you go today, instead of taking an elevator or escalator.

---

* See Romans 12:1, 1 Corinthians 6:20, 2 Corinthians 9:7, Mark 10:30,
 Philippians 1:20, Philippians 3:14, Colossians 2:19, Isaiah 40:29–31,
 Romans 12:2.

Get Bitter or Get Better

Lindsay Roberts

Watch out that no bitterness takes root among you,
for as it springs up it causes deep trouble,
hurting many in their spiritual lives.
—Hebrews 12:15 TLB

Throughout my miscarriages and losing my precious son after just thirty-six hours, I repeatedly had to choose whether I was going to get *bitter and be destroyed* or get *better and let God take over.* It was a decision that only I could make, and I knew that once I made the choice, there would be no turning back. If I was going to get better, I had to believe in what I was doing and never let go. Otherwise, I knew that the grief, anxiety, and hurt would eat me alive.

In your trials you, too, must recognize the fine line between getting bitter and getting better and decide which way you are going to go. This is not an area in which you can "straddle the fence" or change sides. Bitterness will tear you up and do permanent damage unless you make the choice to grab it and take control of it.

At one point, it hit me like a ton of bricks that God was my God no matter what happened, not just if He healed me or my children. I had to follow Isaiah 43:18–19: "Forget the former things; do not dwell on the past. See, I am doing a new thing!"

It is not easy, but once you decide not to get bitter, it will be your day of new beginnings as it was for me.[18]

make **your** day count

Are you harboring bitterness inside about a wrong that was done to you, a disappointment you have faced? God is still God, and He wants to give you a new beginning. Give Him that bitterness today, and then get ready for the good things He will do.

Secrets I Helped My Husband Learn

Evelyn Roberts

A wife of noble character who can find?
She is worth far more than rubies.
—Proverbs 31:10

Oral says he has learned some helpful secrets from me. Perhaps you can benefit from them as well.

1. Put family first. When our healing ministry began, Oral was so busy that he didn't have much time to spend with our children, and it showed. I encouraged him to change this because I was concerned the children weren't going to know him when they were grown. Oral began spending more time with each child doing whatever they enjoyed. Family comes before ministry and work.

2. Control your reactions. I encouraged Oral to be calm and first tell people all the good things they had done before discussing where they had fallen short.

3. Use good grammar. Since Oral was going to be talking to millions of people, together we took a correspondence refresher course in grammar. I think he speaks almost perfect English now.

4. Learn to receive. It was difficult for Oral to receive the harvest resulting from our seeds of faith. I told him, "If we don't receive what God gives back to us, then we can't teach the people how to receive what God wants to give back to them." Ever since that time, the Lord has given us outstanding harvests because of the seeds of faith we've planted. It's part of the Bible, and it works![19]

make **your** day count

Do any of these areas strike you as needing improvement in your own life or in that of your spouse? Or is there some other area that needs your attention? Begin by making some small change today.

time **saving** tips

Tips to Make Your Day Count

You can line the inside doors of your kitchen cabinets with self-stick cork tiles and turn them into bulletin boards. They are great for holding take-out menus, favorite recipes, emergency telephone numbers, and more.[20]

A great way to enjoy the photos you receive from family and loved ones at Christmas is to mount a bulletin board in a place where you will see it often, then neatly organize the photos on it. Each Christmas, remove the photos from the previous year and begin putting up new ones.

Try using straight pins instead of thumbtacks and pushpins to hang photos on a bulletin board. The pins don't detract from the photos, yet they do the trick.

Simple Rice Pilaf[21]

Evelyn Roberts

1 pkg. dry chicken noodle soup mix
2 cups water
1 cup dry rice (uncooked), preferably brown rice
2 Tbsp. margarine

In a pot put the water and the flavor packet from the package of dry soup. Bring to a boil.

In a skillet sauté the noodles in the margarine until golden brown.

Remove from heat and pour in dry rice. Stir and let it soak up remainder of margarine.

Put both soup mixture and rice/noodle mixture in casserole with lid on.

Place in 350° oven for 1 hour. Do not stir.

If you use brown rice, it may take an extra 15 minutes to become tender.

Note: This is a recipe my family has enjoyed for many years. Very simple. Can be used with many things: chicken, steak, pork chops, beef, etc.

Having "The Talk"

Taffi L. Dollar

God wants you to be holy and pure and to keep clear of all
sexual sin so that each of you will marry in holiness and
honor—not in lustful passion as the heathen do, in their
ignorance of God and his ways.

—1 Thessalonians 4:4–5 TLB

Everywhere teenagers turn, images of sex are in their
faces. Many think it's "un-cool" to be a virgin. They don't
have any qualms about dating more than one person at a
time or having multiple sexual partners in high school. We
are to show our children that what their peers think is acceptable is unacceptable in God's eyes.

It is important that you sit down with your kids and have
"the talk" before they hit puberty and start noticing boys and
girls. This will be one of the most important discussions you
ever have with them. When you tell them about sex outside
of marriage and it's possible consequences (pregnancy and
sexually transmitted diseases), include what the Bible has to
say about intercourse.

Your children may think that the Bible is an out-of-date
book that has little relevance to what's going on in the world
today; however, explain that it is the living Word of God and
that God is the same yesterday, today, and forever. (Heb.
13:8.) What was written in the Bible still applies to our lives

today. In fact, Paul said, "Whatsoever things were written aforetime were written for our learning" (Rom. 15:4 KJV). Teach your children that sex is a gift, and when it is enjoyed in the confines of a godly marriage, it is a blessing indeed.[22]

make **your** day count

Regardless of the ages of your children, you can begin praying about their sexuality today and discussing age-appropriate information. Ask God for wisdom as to when to have "the talk" and how to go about it so that it will have the maximum impact.

Protected by the Blood of Jesus

Kellie Copeland Kutz

They overcame him by the blood of the Lamb
and by the word of their testimony.
—Revelation 12:11

Shortly after my cousin Nikki, an on-fire-for-God believer, was killed in an accident involving a drunk driver, I began to seek the Lord to find out how we could make sure this never happened again. That very week, I heard Billye Brim teach on the blood of Jesus, stressing, "We have to plead the blood of Jesus over our families every morning and every night."

As I began to study the Bible on the subject, I read about God supernaturally protecting the Israelites from the plagues sent against Pharaoh and his people for refusing to let God's people go. In Exodus 12, God instituted the Passover to protect the Israelites from the final judgment on the Egyptians: the death of every firstborn.

In Exodus 12:7, God instructed the Israelites to "take of the blood, and strike it on the two side posts and on the upper door post of the houses (KJV)." Those who obeyed were protected behind the blood and escaped death. Today, we can apply the blood of Jesus to the "doorposts" of our lives by speaking words of faith.

God is offering us assurance that our loved ones will be protected. We do this by walking in the light of God's Word and appropriating His promise of protection through the blood of Jesus.[23]

make **your** day count

Present yourself and those you love to the Lord today, striking the doorposts of your lives with the blood of Jesus through prayer. Reading the account of the Passover in Exodus 12 will strengthen and encourage your faith.

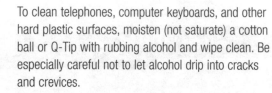

time **saving** tips

Uses for Rubbing Alcohol

Betsy Williams

To clean telephones, computer keyboards, and other hard plastic surfaces, moisten (not saturate) a cotton ball or Q-Tip with rubbing alcohol and wipe clean. Be especially careful not to let alcohol drip into cracks and crevices.

Rubbing alcohol also works to remove that stubborn adhesive residue (from price tags or other labels) on glass, plastic, and china. (To be on the safe side, test an inconspicuous area first.) Apply with cotton and "thumb roll" the adhesive into balls and remove.

Ants in a Boat

Cleo Justus

This is a nice low sugar after school snack. It would be nice to have the celery prepared ahead of time and on a low shelf where children can reach it themselves. Place the raisins and cream cheese nearby.

Wash and cut celery sticks into 6-inch pieces.

Lay on paper towel to dry.

Spread hollow inside of celery stick with cream cheese and top with raisins.

Step by Step to Victory

Julie Wilson

In his heart a man plans his course,
but the LORD determines his steps.
—Proverbs 16:9

Lindsay Roberts and I have been longtime friends. Many years ago we both delivered babies at the same time at what was then the City of Faith hospital in Tulsa, Oklahoma. Afterward, Lindsay went in for her well-baby checkup and everything was fine. My well-baby checkup was with the same doctor, but my baby was not fine. In fact, we were told that he had cancer and a liver that was seven times larger than normal.

Times like this are why we must have a personal relationship with the Lord. I didn't have a clue that the diagnosis was coming, but it was no surprise to God. I praise God for the doctors that helped my child, but they didn't know the perfect plan. Only God knew that. Doctors often know what works, but only God knew for sure what would work for my son. The doctors gave their diagnosis, but we appealed to the higher court of God's final judgment.

We asked God to show us the perfect path through the trial and to help us walk in it. That is the only thing that produces victory. We chose to utilize the best that medicine had to offer, while at the same time, we continued to pray. So many people prayed and stood in faith with us, and God healed my son.

Ask God to reveal His perfect path to your victory. Step by step, follow it, and you will win.[24]

make **your** day count

Ask the Lord to show you the next step in your miracle journey.
Take that one step today!

A Mother by Blessing

Pat Harrison

From infancy you have known the holy Scriptures,
which are able to make you wise for salvation
through faith in Christ Jesus.
—2 Timothy 3:15

You are a woman by birth and a wife by choice, but you are a mother by blessing. As your children's parent, it is your responsibility to provide a spiritual heritage for them. Proverbs 22:6 says, "Train a child in the way he should go, and when he is old he will not turn from it." Children must be trained to live the Christian life.

Loving Jesus was always a way of life for me. All the memories I have of my childhood are within the context of a home that was full of love because God was there. It was a place where the Word of God was continually being read, taught, and experienced. Because of that, when I became a teenager, I could never drift too far away from my spiritual roots.

From the time your children are born, their spirits are alive unto God. When you talk to them about Jesus and share God's Word from the beginning, spiritual things will become as natural to them as earthly things are to other children. When your children fall down and get scraped, they'll know that the first thing to do is pray. God will be real to them because God's Word has been planted in their hearts.[25]

make **your** day count

Be alert to any needs your children may have today, and pray with them
about those matters right on the spot. As you incorporate this
practice into your everyday living, it will become the natural thing
for your children to do to involve God in their lives.

The Family Covenant

Marilyn Hickey

*Blessed is the man who fears the L*ORD*,*
who finds great delight in his commands.
His children will be mighty in the land;
the generation of the upright will be blessed.
Wealth and riches are in his house.

—Psalm 112:1–3

Because you are in covenant relationship with God and your mate, you have the right to claim God's promises for your children. Isaiah 54:13 KJV says, "All thy children shall be taught of the LORD; and great shall be the peace of thy children." God is concerned about the peace of your children.

He wants to bless you and your family, but you must "choose life" for yourself and for them as instructed in Deuteronomy 30:19. Life is the result of living according to God's Word.

Our text states that your children are supposed to be mighty. It's not enough to see them just make it into heaven; they are to be mighty in the land. The passage goes on to say that wealth and riches will be in your house and in your children's house. God wants to bless your home with abundant provision. It is part of your covenant.

According to Proverbs 24:15, the wicked can't touch the house of the righteous because God's Word is there. And in another passage it says, "The house of the wicked shall be overthrown: but the tabernacle of the upright shall flourish" (Prov. 14:11 KJV). You and your family have a covenant relationship with God that will cause you to flourish. Receive all the blessings that go with the covenant, and don't settle for anything less.[26]

make **your** day count

Give God thanks today for His covenant promises for you and your family.
Thank Him for causing the peace of your children to be great,
for making them mighty in the earth, and for supplying the
needs of your family with His abundant provision.

Seed-Faith Living

Evelyn Roberts

[Jesus said], "The kingdom of heaven is like a mustard seed, which a man took and planted in his field. Though it is the smallest of all your seeds, yet when it grows, it is the largest of garden plants and becomes a tree."
—Matthew 13:31–32

Young children can grasp faith concepts at an early age. Once I spoke to a third-grade class about seed-faith living. I planted some seeds in a planter and took it to the class, so they could watch the plants grow. I explained that the good seeds I had planted would become flowers, but if the seeds were bad, they would see a weed or nothing at all. I explained that I had planted the seeds, but only God could make them grow.

Then I told them that every day they, too, were planting seeds—either good seeds, like doing something kind for another, or bad seeds, like saying something unkind. "Ask God to help you plant good seeds," I told them, "so good can come back to you." By introducing your children to seed-faith living, you can help them receive the breakthroughs they need in their lives.

God wants us to raise our children according to His Word. In Isaiah 59:21, the Lord says, "My Spirit, who is on you, and my words that I have put in your mouth will not depart from your mouth, or from the mouths of your children, or from the mouths of their descendants from this time on and forever." This is God's promise that the seeds of faith we plant in our children will produce fruit.[27]

make **your** day count

Find a Bible promise that covers an area of need in your family, and share it with your children. Each of you plant that promise as a seed today by thinking about it and saying it to yourselves.

time **saving** tips

Uses for Plastic Grocery Bags

Betsy Williams

You know that multitude of plastic grocery bags you have that seem to multiply like rabbits? Here are some ways you can put them to work for you:

 Each evening before the kids get ready for bed, give them each one of the bags to collect all of their hats, toys, books, etc. Anything that belongs in their rooms goes into the bags and to their rooms.

 Line small wastebaskets with them. When it's time to empty the trash, tie the handles and toss.

When cooking, hang one of the bags from a drawer or cabinet knob. You can also close a drawer on one of the handles. As you prepare your meal, put all scraps and waste in the bag. When you are finished cooking, tie the handles and throw away.

 These plastic bags can be stuffed inside a tube from a paper towel roll and stored in a drawer or in the car, making them readily available when you need them.

 Put meat scraps, meat trays, or other items that can smell up the trashcan in these bags. It's a good idea to use two bags, one inside another, to prevent leaks. Tie the handles and store in the freezer until trash day.

Caterpillar Fun Snack

Cleo Justus

These are fun to make and fun to eat!

Take a handful of small Ritz Crackers.

Spread cream cheese or peanut butter between them, adding on to make a long caterpillar.

Spread cream cheese or peanut butter on front and add two raisins for eyes.

So Your Kids Want to Date?

Taffi L. Dollar

The steps of a good man are ordered by the LORD,
and He delights in his way.
—Psalm 37:23 NKJV

It may sound strange to your children, but God wants to be involved in their relationships, especially dating. He wants to show them how to dress, what to say, and whom to date. It isn't a sin to date, but it is a sin to get into a relationship without involving God. Before your children can learn to establish a relationship with other people, they must have a good relationship with Him.

Encourage your children to spend time with the Lord by reading and studying the Bible daily. As they develop a relationship with God and allow Him to direct them, He will lead them to their future mates.

How can God be interested in dating? In Genesis 2:18 He said that it was not good for Adam to be alone. Did Adam search for a wife? No. God brought Eve to him. Tell your teenagers to stop wasting their time by looking for someone on their own. God knows their likes and dislikes. By their having a good, solid relationship with Him, He will speak to their hearts not only about dating but also about their education, friendships, and other areas that are important to them.[28]

make **your** day count

Talk with your children about dating and getting emotionally involved with someone of the opposite sex. Pray and encourage your children to pray about involving God in all of their relationships, especially dating.

Take Advantage of Angelic Protection

Kellie Copeland Kutz

Bless the LORD, you His angels,
Who excel in strength, who do His word,
Heeding the voice of His word.
—Psalm 103:20 NKJV

If we are going to protect every area of our lives and the lives of those we love, we must understand and appropriate the angelic ministry. According to Hebrews 1:14, angels are servants sent to minister for us because we are heirs of salvation.

We may seem insignificant when we compare ourselves to angels, but God doesn't see it that way. Hebrews 2:5–6 explains that angels are not placed higher than us spiritually. He sent them to helpfully care for and look after us!

Because of this, God has given us the authority to command our angels to act on our behalf. Therefore, it is very important that you watch what comes out of your mouth. Make sure that your words reflect God's Word, because your angels were created to obey it.

Charge the angels to go forth on your behalf and that of your family. Pray, "I charge you, angels, in the name of Jesus, to watch over my children and my loved ones today—to go before them, to protect them, and to keep them from all harm!" Then make sure you don't speak any negative words that would bind the angels' hands from helping you! God wants to protect you and the ones you love.[29]

make **your** day count

Look up the two passages in Hebrews mentioned above and reflect
on what they mean to you. Then charge the angels
to go forth to keep you and your loved ones safe.

Just Say Yes!

Lindsay Roberts

No matter how many promises God has made,
they are "Yes" in Christ.
—2 Corinthians 1:20

When I was eighteen, I was told that I would never have children. Today I have three daughters—all miracles—but they did not come easily. Before I received my miracles, I had miscarriages, a tumor, surgeries, and the death of a baby son.

I finally had to come to a place that instead of saying, "God heals people," I had to say, "God heals *me.*" It was when I made a decision to believe God's promise of healing for myself that the miracles began.

In John 5:1–15, Jesus approached a man who had been waiting thirty-eight years by the Pool of Bethesda for an angel to stir the water so he could be healed. In thirty-eight years, the man had not figured out how to be the first into the pool to be healed! He was just waiting and wondering.

Jesus asked him, "Do you want to get well?" (v. 6). Instead of saying yes, the man replied, "I have no one to [put] me into the pool" (v. 7). Jesus looked for people who would answer, "Yes! I believe!"

Today we have the same opportunity. Instead of saying, "I don't have anyone to help me," or, "God heals people, but

He hasn't healed me," we must say, "Yes! I believe I receive my healing." Then we must stay expectant in faith until the miracle comes.[30]

make **your** day count

Whatever miracle you need today, know that God wants to perform it. Talk to God, saying, "Yes! I believe Your promise concerning my need. Yes, You are talking to me!"

Healthful Food Substitutions[31]

Try some of these substitutions to replace fattening, less healthy ingredients in some of your favorite recipes:

INGREDIENT	SUBSTITUTE
Butter	Canola oil, mild olive oil, prune puree, or applesauce
1 ounce chocolate	3 Tbsp. cocoa
Cream or whole milk in batters, muffins, or biscuit doughs	Skim, low-fat, or 1% milk
Cream cheese	Low-fat ricotta + yogurt
Cream cheese in cheesecake	½ whole-milk ricotta + either part-skim ricotta or low-fat (1%) cottage cheese
Sour cream	Plain yogurt
Whipped cream, ice cream to top cakes, pies, warm fruit desserts	Frozen yogurt or low-fat yogurt
1 cup heavy or whipping cream	1 cup evaporated skim milk

Lindsay's Favorite Chicken Wings[32]

Lindsay Roberts

2 lbs. chicken wings
$\frac{1}{2}$ cup brown sugar
$\frac{1}{2}$ cup granulated sugar
$\frac{1}{2}$ cup soy sauce
1 cup chicken broth

Wash chicken, pat dry, and set aside.

In baking dish, mix all other ingredients and add chicken. Be
sure all pieces are well coated and cover.

Refrigerate to marinate for at least 2 hours. I prefer marinating
overnight. Does not taste the same when marinated in
less time.

Bake uncovered at 400° for 45 minutes. Serve warm or cold.

The Body/Finance Connection

Marty Copeland

*Present your bodies a living sacrifice, holy, acceptable
to God, which is your reasonable service.*
—Romans 12:1 NKJV

The prosperity of your body is as much a part of your covenant as the prosperity of your finances. Health and wealth are spiritually linked. It's what I call the body/finance connection.

One afternoon, as I was praying for people's deliverance from food addiction, the Lord dropped these words into my heart: *Trying to lose weight without presenting your body as a living sacrifice is like trying to prosper financially without tithing. It just won't work.*

God's Word says there are three things that belong to God: your spirit, your body, and your tithe. First Corinthians 6:19–20 states that your body is the temple of the Holy Spirit and you are not your own. You are bought with a price.

Why does God ever ask anything of us? So He can get something to us. Submitting your spirit to the lordship of Jesus gives you eternal life. Submitting your tithes and offerings to God gives you prosperity. As you submit your body to God as a living sacrifice, you are giving your first fruits, so all the rest will be blessed. He will get involved in your eating habits; He will get involved in your weight loss.

Health and prosperity are part of your covenant. Grab hold of them! You've got the right—the covenant right![33]

make **your** day count

Pray, "God, you live inside me. I have my body because of You, and it's not my own. I've been bought with the price of Your dear Son. Father, I submit my body to You as a living sacrifice. Thank You for blessing it."

Loving Discipline

Pat Harrison

*Discipline your son while there is hope, but do not
[indulge your angry resentments by undue
chastisements and] set yourself to his ruin.*
—Proverbs 19:18 AMP

Proverbs 13:24 is clear: "He who loves [his son] is careful to discipline him." And there is a proper way to do it. You do not do it in anger or because of resentment you might be harboring. You discipline because you love your children. You see their errors, and you want to teach them right from wrong, so they can be loving and obedient.

We are to calm ourselves down and let the love that is within us flow forth to our children; then we can discipline them properly. If you try to correct them in anger, you run a high risk of disciplining incorrectly. For instance, perhaps you feel frustrated over something, and right then your child does something wrong that triggers frustration. It would be easy to take out that frustration on your child.

My father never disciplined my brother or me in any way without sitting us down and asking us, "Do you understand why you are being punished?" He would make us tell him what we had done wrong and why we were being disciplined. If we did not answer correctly, he would explain our offense to us, then we would receive our punishment. We respected our parents as a result. They set a good example for us to follow.[34]

make **your** day count

When it comes to disciplining your children today, wait till you are in a calm frame of mind, even if it means putting off the discipline for a while. Use the opportunity to teach godly principles from the Bible.

Loving the Woman in the Mirror

Taffi L. Dollar

*[We] continued to behold [in the Word of God] as
in a mirror the glory of the Lord, are constantly being
transfigured into His very own image.*
—2 Corinthians 3:18 AMP

God has a specific assignment for you. Your ability to
fulfill this plan, however, depends on how you see yourself.
Your self-image must line up with God's image in order for
you to successfully accomplish His purpose for your life.

You must make a decision. Do you want to look and live
like the world or conform to God's ideal image of you? Is
your self-perception based on someone else's opinion of you
or God's opinion? We should be more concerned about what
God thinks and learn to appreciate the woman He has made
us to be.

We can learn a lot from Adam and Eve. Although they
were perfectly created in God's image, they weren't satisfied.
They wanted to improve what God had already made perfect.
Genesis 1:26 tells us that God made us in His image, after
His likeness, but Adam and Eve lost sight of this truth.

The serpent conned them into thinking that God had
short-changed them. He said, "God knows that when you eat

of it your eyes will be opened, and you will be like God" (Gen. 3:5). The truth is, Adam and Eve were *already* like God!

Are you attempting to become what you already are? You should never be ashamed of the woman you see in the mirror. You are beautiful in God's eyes, created in His image! Begin to see yourself that way.[35]

make **your** day count

Look in the mirror today, and affirm that you are made in God's image, after His likeness. God loves the woman He sees. Do you? If not, ask God to help you see yourself like He does.

If I Could Do It Again

Evelyn Roberts

Don't be fools; be wise: make the most of every opportunity
you have for doing good. Don't act thoughtlessly, but try to
find out and do whatever the Lord wants you to.
—Ephesians 5:16–17 TLB

Looking back over the rearing of my children, I've asked myself if I had a second chance to go back and do it again what would I change?

First, I'd spend more time together as a family. The long-term benefits of time spent together far outweigh any special sacrifices required on occasion by individual family members to make that time possible.

Second, even though we prayed with our children and read Scriptures to them, I would do it twice as much. You can never get too much of the Word of God into your children. And when it is presented in an interesting, appetizing way, it can be very beneficial, especially in their future years.

Third, I would spend more time just loving them and building them up in their self-confidence.

We get only one chance at rearing our children. So those of you who have children at home, do all you can to promote the love of Jesus in their hearts. Remember that children are really just with us as we pass through this life.

Although there are many things that we can and should do for them to make this present life the best one possible, the most important thing that we can ever do is to help them prepare their hearts and their souls to someday spend eternity with Jesus.[36]

make **your** day count

Evaluate where you stand in these three areas. Choose one to concentrate on today and make the investment in your children's lives.

time **saving** tips

Car Travel Games for Kids

Betsy Williams

Road trips can provide a great opportunity for quality time together. Having fun as a family not only creates happy memories, it also makes a long drive much more enjoyable.

 Count Volkswagen Beetles. Green ones count as an extra point.

 Print maps of the United States off the Internet. As you spot license plates from the various states, let the kids color in those states on their maps.

 Learn how to do string tricks such a Jacob's Ladder and Cat's in the Cradle. Simple instructions with illustrations can be found on several Web sites.

 Look for letters of the alphabet from A to Z on signs, billboards, license tags, and buildings. The first person to reach Z wins.

 Play I Spy for things inside the vehicle.

 Play Who Am I Thinking About. One person thinks of a person or character who can be real or fictional, dead or alive. Bugs Bunny, for example. The other people ask yes/no questions to try to figure out whom the person or character is. Whoever guesses first gets to think of the next person or character.

Ants on a Log

Cleo Justus

This is a wonderful after-school snack that children can prepare for themselves. It might be helpful to wash and cut the celery ahead of time and place in a plastic bag on a lower refrigerator shelf.

Wash and cut celery stocks into 6-inch pieces.

Lay on paper towel to dry.

Spread top side of celery with peanut butter and top
    with raisins.

Breaking Generational Curses

Marilyn Hickey

Know therefore that the LORD your God is God; he is the
faithful God, keeping his covenant of love to a thousand
generations of those who love him and keep his commands.
—Deuteronomy 7:9

Robert was destined for failure. I'm sure if we examined his family tree, we would discover generations of his family that either became caught up in a cycle of destructive behavior or, like Robert, were born into it. The good news is that Robert heard the life-changing Word of the Gospel and broke this pattern of behavior by accepting Christ. The bad news is that there are many traits in our families—illnesses, attitudes, behavioral characteristics—that are passed down from generation to generation, and few people know how to change this destructive trend.

God wants to shed light on the hidden causes of defeat in our families and root out stubborn and seeming impasses. As we apply the truth of God's Word to our personal lives, we will establish a tradition of blessing for our present and future generations—a life of abundance, fulfillment, and victory in Christ—for our children, our children's children, and the next generation.

There are two sides of the same coin. Exodus 20:5 says, "I the LORD thy God am a jealous God, visiting the iniquity of the fathers upon the children unto the third and fourth generation of them that hate me KJV." The other side? Our text states that for those who love God and keep His commandments, He keeps His covenant and mercy, for a thousand generations![37]

make **your** day count

Take to God whatever negative traits have been passed down through your family, and break the power of them in Jesus' name.*
Exchange them in prayer for God's covenant and mercy for you, your children, and the generations to follow.

---

* See Matthew 18:18.

Protection by Listening to Your Spirit

Kellie Copeland Kutz

Your ears will hear a word behind you, saying,
This is the way; walk in it.
—Isaiah 30:21 AMP

When it comes to protecting your children and those you love, it is so important to learn to listen to your spirit. God is always speaking to us. I don't believe one calamity ever happens to us that the Holy Spirit doesn't speak to our spirits beforehand to warn us. John 16:13 says that the Spirit of truth will show us things to come. He knows what the enemy is trying to do. If we are in tune with His voice, He can protect us from the devil's attacks.

I strongly encourage you to pray what I prayed: "Lord, I want to be able to hear You when You speak to me. I want to know what You sound like." God took me to school after I prayed that prayer! He put me through one little exercise after another, and His training caused me to grow light-years in my spiritual walk!

First Peter 5:8 tells us to be sober and vigilant because the enemy walks about as a roaring lion, seeking whom he may devour. Be ever watchful. Keep your spiritual antenna up, always listening on the inside for the Holy Spirit's leading. As you listen to your spirit and heed the Holy Spirit's voice, you can make sure the enemy never has the opportunity to devour you or your family![38]

make **your** day count

Ask God to teach you to recognize and heed His voice.
Write down the impressions and thoughts you have.
Often this is God's way of speaking to you, although it should be noted that He will never tell us things that are contrary to His Word.
Ask Him to help you discern between your thoughts and His.

Don't Get Stressed Out, Stand Still!

Lindsay Roberts

Fear ye not, stand still, and see the salvation of the LORD.
—Exodus 14:13 KJV

Are you so overwhelmed by everything you need to accomplish that you feel as though you might crack? I understand what it's like to be stressed. It's difficult to find balance in our lives with our hectic schedules and multitude of responsibilities.

Fear is a major cause of stress, yet there are many places in the Bible where God tells us to "fear not." When we "fear not," we are able to step outside the realm of being panic-stricken by circumstances. Then we are to "stand still."

Have you ever tried to make sense to a person who is running around all stressed out? In contrast, if you will stand still and get into an atmosphere of faith, you will "see the salvation of the Lord."

When I looked up this Scripture in the original text, I found that it means, "One who comes from outside to bring help." When you're in the middle of a stressful situation, the problems are often all you can see. Of course, if you were in the middle of a fire, the situation would look really bad to you. But if you were *outside* the fire, you would be able to handle it more rationally. God deals with your circumstances from outside the stress, so step outside with Him. He has the solution you need![39]

make **your** day count

Make a conscious effort to "step out of" your circumstances today.
Stand still with God outside those circumstances,
and watch as He saves the day.

time **saving** tips

Stress Busters

Betsy Williams

Breathe. Take ten deep breaths through your mouth, exhaling slowly through your nose.

Close your eyes and for sixty seconds, reflect on one of your most enjoyable experiences. It could be something like a family vacation, a favorite Christmas from childhood, or holding your baby for the first time.

Take the scenic route.

Pet an animal.

Sing!

Listen to classical music.

Eat slowly and actually taste your food.

Lindsay's Goulash[40]

Lindsay Roberts

1 1/2 cups macaroni
2 lbs. extra lean ground beef or ground turkey
2 large onions, chopped
2 large cans of tomatoes
Canola oil

Cook macaroni according to package directions. Drain and set aside.

In a frying pan lightly coated with canola oil, brown the onions until they are transparent. Remove from pan and set aside.

In same frying pan, brown the ground meat until completely cooked. Drain off all fat.

Add the onions, macaroni, and canned tomatoes, juice and all.

Simmer until all ingredients are heated thoroughly.

Your Seeds Will Produce a Harvest in Your Children

Evelyn Roberts

[Jesus] told them another parable: "The kingdom of heaven is like a mustard seed, which a man took and planted in his field. Though it is the smallest of all your seeds, yet when it grows, it is the largest of garden plants and becomes a tree, so that the birds of the air come and perch in its branches."

—Matthew 13:31–32

We are not always permitted to see the visible results of the seeds planted in the hearts of our children, but we have the promise from God's Word that there will be a time of harvest. If you bring your children under the guidance of the Holy Spirit, with Jesus Christ at the center of your life, God assures you that even if your children go astray, they've got to come back. They may not accept Jesus when they're young, but when they're old, they will.

I once read about a saloon proprietor who heard a sermon on the evils of drinking and gambling. He was converted and closed his saloon. He said the sermon reminded him of the teaching he had received at his mother's knee. It had never really lost its hold on him even though it had lain dormant in his heart for years.

You may be starting late to apply God's principles of training. Your children may be older—and even rebellious. But don't give up. Start now to pray for them and to live a godly life before them. There is a promise in the Bible for you: "With God nothing shall be impossible" (Luke 1:37 KJV).[41]

make **your** day count

What godly seed could you plant in your children's lives today? The seed could be in the form of words or from your example. Talk to God about it, and He'll lead you. Then continue to water those seeds through your prayer.

Teaching Your Children to Behave in Public

Pat Harrison

A wise son brings joy to his father,
but a foolish son grief to his mother.
—Proverbs 10:1

It is important for parents to teach their children how to dress and behave in public. My brother and I did not always have many clothes, but what we had was always clean and put together properly. My mother never let us go out of the house if we did not look nice.

I grew up in a minister's home, so sometimes we would go to lunch with the ministers for whom my dad was preaching. I remember my mother asking some of these parents, "Would you like me to help you get your children ready to go?"

"Oh, we're not going to take them," they would reply. "They don't act like your children in public."

When my parents said to sit still, I knew they meant what they said. So no matter what I was doing at that moment, if they told me to stop, I stopped and sat still. I understood that they were the authority and that I was to respect that fact.

It is so important to teach children these things early if at all possible, because it will never get any easier. If your children are older, take heart and begin now. God will give you the wisdom you need, and He will work in your children's hearts.[42]

make **your** day count

Think of one area of discipline in which your children need to improve. Find out what the Bible says about that issue, then discuss it with your children, letting them know what you expect and what the consequence will be if they violate that principle. Then follow through.

The First Date

Taffi L. Dollar

Treat younger men as brothers, older women as mothers,
and younger women as sisters, with absolute purity.

—1 Timothy 5:1–2

Many parents wonder what is the right age for dating. I think it depends on the child's maturity. I also don't think that they need to rush into dating because of all of the emotions that are involved.

If you allow your children to begin dating at a young age, they will also learn the cycle of breaking up and moving on to another person. This cycle only prepares them for divorce. How? They've learned that if they aren't satisfied or like where a relationship is going, instead of trying to work it out, they can leave.

A healthy, romantic relationship can only be built on the firm foundation of friendship. By first developing a friendship with the opposite sex, your child can enjoy the person's company without any pressure. Friendship will last even if the boyfriend/girlfriend relationship doesn't.

My husband, Creflo, regularly takes our daughters out on dates. He opens the door for them and treats them like ladies. He does this so that when they do start dating, they will know the manner in which they should be treated by men—with love, honor, and respect. If the young men don't treat them the same way their dad does, they know the guys aren't worthy of their time. Parents, I encourage you to do the same with your children.[43]

make **your** day count

Make a date with each of your children, one at a time. Spend part of that time teaching them how to treat the opposite sex and how they can expect to be treated. Talk to them about having respect for themselves and others. Practice manners and good communication skills.

Establishing Your Priorities

Sharon Daugherty

Teach us to number our days and recognize how few
they are; help us to spend them as we should.
—Psalm 90:12 TLB

God's priorities should be what we seek in life. If we follow His plan, we'll walk with proper balance in all of our responsibilities. Establish what things are most important, then let everything else fall into its right place. I've found the following guidelines, in this order, to be helpful: time with God, time with husband, time with family, and time for ministering to others.

The duties of a wife and mother fall into order as we first submit our ways to God. Time with God is so vital. If we don't have time with Him, we won't be filled up to handle the day effectively. Spiritually speaking, we'll run out of patience, joy, peace, and self-control; and we'll miss God's leading in areas.

On the other hand, if we start our day with prayer and God's Word, we can put on the armor of God, our spirits will be filled with the fruit of the Holy Spirit, and our hearts will be sensitive to hear God's voice speaking to us. (See Eph. 6:11–17 and Gal. 5:22–23.)

Take time to read and study God's Word every day, even if it's only a few minutes. Don't let anything or anyone talk you out of it. Remember, you are in a spiritual battle, and you need to keep your guard up. Your time with God is your source of strength.[44]

make **your** day count

Find a Bible promise each morning to discuss with your children. You can find boxes of promises on cards at Christian bookstores. Then pray with your children, applying the promise to their specific needs. You can do this over breakfast, on the way to school, or at night before bed. Even five minutes will help establish God's Word and prayer as priorities in their lives.

time **saving** tips

Gifts for Students to Give Teachers

 A car wash

 Gift certificate for a book, music, or video

 Gift certificate for manicure or pedicure

 Handmade notes with heartfelt sentiments from parent and child

 Stationery and note cards

 A special pen

 Ask the teacher to write up a wish list of things needed for the classroom and distribute the list to the other parents.

 Science experiment kit such as a butterfly kit

 Soothing music to be played while children do seat work

Computer programs

Board games to be played during recess on rainy days

easy **recipes**

Sausage Balls[45]

Sharon Daugherty

1 lb. sausage
1 lb. mild cheese, grated
3 cups Bisquick mix

Mix with hands; form into walnut-size balls.

Bake at 350° for 10 minutes.

For convenience, these may be frozen prior to baking.

The Four Stages of Friendship

Deborah Butler

Two are better than one, because they have a
good return for their work: If one falls down,
his friend can help him up.
—Ecclesiastes 4:9–10

Friends are a gift from God. But good friendships don't just happen; there is a process involved. I believe there are four stages of friendship: the acquaintance stage, the casual friendship, the close friendship, and the intimate friendship. Each of these stages must be handled correctly in order for the relationship to be godly. We need God's guidance throughout the process.

The acquaintance stage takes place when you first meet someone. An acquaintance becomes a casual friend when you spend time with the person and ask basic questions. At this phase, we have the responsibility to ask God, "Why has this person crossed my path? Did You send him or her?"

Once you have gone through the acquaintance and casual friendship stages with someone, you use the same standards for establishing a close friendship. Here you decide at what level the relationship should stay. If you desire to bring the person further into your life, then you move to the intimate friendship stage, which involves best friends and even marriage.

It is important that we teach our children this process also. After years of practice establishing what type of relationship is or isn't right for them, it will help them in their dating relationships. It will even help them know when they've found the person they are to marry. Friends are a great blessing at every stage.[46]

make **your** day count

Call one of your intimate friends today to let him or her know
how much you appreciate the friendship you share.

Protecting Your Children Through Discipline

Kellie Copeland Kutz

Children, obey your parents in the Lord, for this is right.
"Honor your father and mother...that it may go well
with you and that you may enjoy long life on the earth."
—Ephesians 6:1–3

There's no way around it. The Bible says that if your children are going to live long on the earth, they have to obey their parents. That doesn't just happen automatically. You have to teach them to be obedient, and the only way to do that is to discipline them.

God laid out the perfect system in His Word for disciplining your children. Interestingly, He doesn't even mention "time-outs." Actually, the only form of parental discipline the Word really talks about is spanking—and that's the one kind of discipline the world says not to use!

What amazes me is that so many believers have agreed with secular society on this subject. They say, "Well, the Bible is outdated in its instructions on discipline." Not surprisingly, these Christians are also reaping the same results in their children that secular society is—disobedience, disrespect, and rebellion.

I haven't found any truth in the Bible that has passed away, and that includes God's instructions on parental discipline.

You can't believe God for something apart from His Word. You have to obey what His Word says; only then are you in a position to believe God for the desired results—children who grow up to be obedient, respectful, a lot of fun, and continually protected from harm.[47]

make **your** day count

Go over Ephesians 6:1–3 with your children. Teach them that there is great reward when they honor and obey you—long life on the earth.

A Word about Your Children

Gloria Copeland

I will pour out my Spirit on your offspring,
and my blessing on your descendants.
—Isaiah 44:3

Society has much to say about your children these days—
most of it is bad. We're being told their economic futures are
bleak, their ethics are waning, and, for the most part, they're
on a downward slide.

But if you've made Jesus Lord of your life, God has something very different to say about your children. He says
they're headed for heaven, not hell; a blessing, not a curse. So
ignore secular society and trust the Bible. It has the power to
turn your children's lives around! Take these verses to heart:

"This is what the Lord says: 'Restrain your voice from
weeping and your eyes from tears, for your work will be
rewarded,' declares the Lord. 'They will return from the land
of the enemy. So there is hope for your future,' declares the
Lord. 'Your children will return to their own land'" (Jer.
31:16–17).

"The desire of the righteous is only good" (Prov. 11:23 KJV).

"I will contend with those who contend with you, and
your children I will save" (Isa. 49:25).

"I will pour water on the thirsty land, and streams on the dry ground; I will pour out my Spirit on your offspring, and my blessing on your descendants" (Isa. 44:3).[48]

If you are a believer and willing to trust God for the deliverance and salvation of your children, you will not be disappointed.[49]

make **your** day count

Use the verses above as prayers to God on behalf of your children.
The Father loves your children even more than you do, and
He will answer your prayers and honor His promises to you.

time **saving** tips

A Gift from the Kitchen

Purchase several quart-size canning jars, the kind with the ringed lids and round inserts. Get your favorite chocolate chip cookie recipe and layer all of the dry ingredients in the jar. First mix the flour, baking soda, and salt, and pour into the bottom of the jar. The next layer should be the brown sugar, then the white sugar on top of that. Finally, fill the remainder of the jar with chocolate chips.

Next, cut out seven-inch fabric squares, using pinking shears as a nice touch. If the gifts are for Christmas, use Christmas fabric, for instance. Place the round inserts on top of the jars, then center the fabric over them. Screw the rings on top of all.

On a small card, write out the remaining ingredients as well as the instructions for mixing and baking. Punch a hole in the upper left-hand corner of the card and attach it to the lid of the jar with ribbon, raffia, or elastic cording.

Susan's Strawberry Jell-O®⁵⁰

Gloria Copeland

2 small pkgs. Strawberry Banana Jell-O® (or 1 large)
1 ½ cups boiling water
3 or 4 bananas, mashed
1 12-oz. can crushed pineapple, reserving ½ cup juice
1 10-oz. pkg. frozen strawberries
1 cup pecans (optional)

Combine ingredients and refrigerate until firm, then
add topping.

Topping:
8 oz. sour cream
8 oz. Cool Whip®

Mix sour cream and Cool Whip® together and spread over top
of Jell-O®.

A Blessed Family Tree

Marilyn Hickey

I will sing of the LORD's great love forever;
with my mouth I will make your faithfulness
known through all generations.

—Psalm 89:1

Nothing touches you more than your children. When you give place to God in your life, you open yourself and your family to His blessing, both now and for generations to come. When you don't give place to God, you subject your family to any generational curses in your family and open their lives to destructive influences. The following story of two American families illustrates this point.[53]

Max Jukes, an atheist, married a godless woman. Some 560 descendants were traced:

- 300 died paupers. Of them were 150 criminals, 7 murderers, 100 drunkards; half the women were prostitutes.

- Max Jukes' descendants cost the United States government more than $1.25 million in nineteenth century dollars.[54]

Jonathan Edwards—a contemporary of Max Jukes and a committed Christian who gave God first place in his life—married a godly woman. Some 1,394 descendants were traced:

- 295 college graduates. Of them, 13 college presidents, 16 professors.

- 3 U. S. senators, 3 state governors, others were sent as ministers to foreign countries.

- 30 judges, 100 lawyers, 1 dean of a law school.

- 75 officers in the military.

- 100 well-known missionaries, preachers, and prominent authors.

- 80 held public office: 3 were mayors of large cities, 1 was the comptroller of the United States Treasury, 1 vice president of the United States.[51]

make **your** day count

Open your heart and home to God today, giving Him first place in your thoughts, your words, your decisions, and your actions. You can be the very catalyst God uses to bring generational blessings to your family.

Humpty Dumpty Sat on a Wall

Lindsay Roberts

He heals the brokenhearted and binds up their wounds.
—Psalm 147:3

Do you remember the nursery rhyme "Humpty Dumpty"?

> Humpty Dumpty sat on a wall;
> Humpty Dumpty had a great fall;
> All the king's horses
> And all the king's men
> Couldn't put Humpty together again.

Here you have a splattered egg, and nobody could help him. What a mess!

If you turn the rhyme around, it may help you understand God and mankind. When God created man, He put him on a wall of His perfect protection in the Garden of Eden. Then sin got into man's eyes, and he couldn't see God. Sin got into his heart, and he couldn't believe God. He fell right off the wall of God's protection. What a mess!

When through Adam all of mankind fell, all the king's horses and all the king's men—all the prophets throughout the Old Testament—did everything they knew to do, but they couldn't put mankind back together again. *It took a king.* In fact, it took more than just a king. It took *the* King. *It took the King of Kings and Lord of Lords—Jesus!*

Without God, our lives are a mess, and nothing in this world can fix us and make us right. But God sent Jesus to rescue us from the powers of darkness. And not only does He fix us, He makes us new. We are complete in Him.[52]

make **your** day count

Is your life broken? Does it seem beyond repair? Jesus is your King of Kings, the One who can make you whole. Come to Him, and let Him not only put you together again, but make you a new person in Christ.

time **saving** tips

Picking Perfect Veggies

 Cauliflower: look for solid heavy heads with bright green leaves. Avoid heads with brown bruises or specks. The size of the head does not indicate quality.

 Carrots: look for straight, rigid, bright orange carrots without cracks or dry spots. Avoid carrots with many small rootlets because they are old.

 Tomatoes: look for plump, well-shaped, fresh tomatoes that have a fairly firm texture and bright color. Avoid bruised, cracked, or soft tomatoes.

 Broccoli: look for firm stalks with deep green or purplish-green heads that are tightly packed. Avoid heads that are light green or have tiny yellow flowers.

 Avocados: they continue to ripen after they've been picked, so you can buy them when firm, and they will soften. They are ripe when they yield to gentle pressure.

 Cabbage: should be firm and heavy for its size. Look for healthy bright leaves free from withering or brown spots.

 Cucumbers: look for ones that are firm, dark in color, and well-shaped. Avoid those that are soft or wrinkled, as well as ones that are beginning to turn yellow.

Nanny's Sweet Potatoes

Julie Lechlider

Ingredients:

4-6 medium sweet potatoes

1 1/2 sticks butter or margarine

2 cups Brown sugar

Directions:

1. Peel sweet potatoes.

2. Cut potatoes into quarters.

3. Boil cut potatoes in water until they are tender. Drain.

4. Melt butter in a skillet.

5. Add the sweet potatoes to the butter and turn them once to coat.

6. Pour brown sugar on top and let it melt down into the potatoes and butter.

7. Cook over low heat until syrup forms.

*Note: You may need to add a little more brown sugar to make more syrup depending on how many potatoes are used. You may also add pancake syrup.

A Double Miracle

Shelley Fenimore

She said to herself, "If only I may touch
His garment, I shall be made well."
—Matthew 9:21 NKJV

One evening my husband and I discovered that our nine-month-old daughter, Whitney, was burning up with a 106-degree temperature. Within moments she went into a fibril seizure and then went limp for several minutes. Blood tests revealed that her blood count was 3.5 when it should have been 14—a very serious situation. A blood transfusion was scheduled one week later, but this concerned us greatly because of what we had heard about blood contamination.

On Friday, we received a prayer cloth from Oral Roberts Ministries. Like the woman with the issue of blood who reached out to Jesus for healing, we used that prayer cloth as our point of contact to reach out for Whitney's healing. She slept with that prayer cloth all weekend, and on Monday, her blood level was back up to 14! She had been healed! Some trying weeks followed, but God brought us through.

Thirteen years later, in 2002, Whitney accompanied a missions team to Mexico, where they encountered a woman who had been blind for three months. Whitney and the others laid hands on the woman, and she instantly received her sight!

Only God knew that Whitney needed her miracle so that years later she could help deliver a miracle to someone else. God sees your future too, so reach out and take the miracle you need today.[53]

make **your** day count

Whatever you need today, find a Bible promise covering that situation.
Then claim that promise as God's personal promise to you,
which is what the Bible is. Your miracle is on its way!

A Life of Abundance

Gloria Copeland

God is able to make all grace (every favor and
earthly blessing) come to you in abundance.
—2 Corinthians 9:8 AMP

Have you ever noticed that you never hear, "Oh my, I have more money than I need"? Such words sound ridiculous in a world ruled by lack, yet as children of God, that is what we *should* be saying!

Jesus said that we're *in* this world, but we're not *of* it. (John 17:15–16.) We belong to the kingdom of God, and it has no shortages. It has an abundant supply of every resource you will ever need.

Years ago when the only abundance Ken and I had was an abundance of needs, the Lord quickened the text verse to me. In the face of our impossible-looking situation, we chose to believe God's Word and began saying, "God is able to make every earthly blessing come to us in abundance!" We started talking about prosperity instead of lack, and we began obeying the promptings of the Holy Spirit where our finances were concerned. Miraculously, eleven months later, we were completely debt free.

Financially, we had been total failures, yet simply because we believed God and obeyed His Word, God was able to supply us not according to the shortages of this world, but according to His riches in glory. If you will dare to believe God's Word and begin talking about it instead of your circumstances, He'll do the same for you and, abundance will be yours.[54]

make **your** day count

Write down the text verse, and throughout the day, read it out loud to yourself. Choose to believe God's promise instead of any lack you may be experiencing. God's truth triumphs over and changes the things on this earth.

Your Ultimate Line of Defense

Dee Simmons

I will not die but live, and will proclaim
what the LORD has done.

—Psalm 118:17

"You have cancer." Those three words are life changing to everyone who hears them. The lump in my breast was discovered during a routine exam in 1987, and although the resulting surgery was successful, the episode was a wake-up call for me.

I had been a churchgoer, prayed daily, and gave generously, but I had wandered from the strong spiritual moorings my parents provided for me. They instilled in me the Word of God and the importance of a personal relationship with Him. I had been blessed with a life of luxury, but now I faced a terrifying truth—without God at the center of my life, I had nothing.

Medically, I recovered quickly, but God's plan for me involved far more. As well as reconnecting with God through a more intimate relationship with Him, I became an avid student of nutrition. I believed that if you took the best from science and the best from nature, the result would be the foundation for a healthy life. *This will become a ministry to people around the world*, God told me, and it has.

Taking charge of our physical health is certainly important, but our ultimate line of defense is to join our spirits with that of the living God. He wants us to be healthy, whole, and strong in every area of our lives.[55]

make **your** day count

Whether you need healing or are experiencing excellent health, determine to put your relationship with God first today by reading His Word and talking to Him. Thank Him for being your ultimate line of defense.

time **saving** tips

Picking Perfect Fruit

Strawberries usually emit a fruit gas, so when picking ripe strawberries, you should be able to smell their sweet flavor.

Grapefruit: choose ones that are heavy for their size, have fully colored skin, and are even, round shapes, usually with flattened ends.

Bananas: they continue to ripen after picking. You can choose bananas at any stage of ripeness.

Peaches: choose firm ones without a hint of green. Look for a yellow or cream tinge beneath the blush. Avoid fruit that is too soft as it is not as tasty. You can buy peaches firm as they will continue to ripen.

Plums: look for full color. If it's a red plum, most of it should be red. If it's black, the surface should be almost entirely black. You can buy firm as they will continue to ripen.

To ripen most fruit, store it in a brown paper bag to trap the fruit gases. This can cause the fruit to ripen up to ten times faster.

Dee's Strawberry Salad[56]

Dee Simmons

Salad:
2 bags salad mix
$\frac{1}{2}$ bag baby spinach
2 pints strawberries, sliced
2 cups Monterey Jack cheese, grated
$\frac{1}{2}$ cup sliced almonds

Dressing:
1 cup olive oil
$\frac{1}{2}$ cup red vinegar
$\frac{1}{8}$ cup sugar
$\frac{1}{2}$ tsp. salt
2 cloves garlic, crushed
$\frac{1}{4}$ tsp. pepper
$\frac{1}{2}$ tsp. paprika

Brown sliced almonds in 350° oven for 2–3 minutes.

Mix salad greens and add almonds, strawberries, and cheese.

Mix dressing; add to salad. Toss and serve.

Take Charge of Stress

Lindsay Roberts

The LORD gives strength to his people;
the LORD blesses his people with peace.
—Psalm 29:11

When my daughter was seven, she entered her first horse-riding competition on a thirty-year-old Arabian horse, whom she was only going to trot around the arena. As proud parents, we were watching from the stands. When they reached the center of the arena, however, it was if the horse realized he was an Arabian. He began cantering like a crazy horse, then took off like a rocket with Chloe bouncing to high heaven.

Richard and I were terrified beyond words and began praying. Meanwhile Chloe was screaming at the top of her lungs, while the horse just ignored her and headed for one of the exits and ran out of the arena!

Richard and I quickly followed, and we could see she had burst into tears. There was no applause, no ribbon. Nothing but humiliation.

Then to our surprise, Chloe grabbed the horse by the bit, jerked his face to hers, looked him straight in the eyes, and said, "Why did you embarrass me like that in front of all these people? Don't you ever do that to me again!"

Somehow she was able to draw from deep within, from that place of inner strength placed there by God Himself.

The lesson? When you react, stress controls you. When you respond with God's deposit deep within you, you take control over stress. If a seven-year-old can do it, we can too![57]

make **your** day count

More than likely, stress will come your way today. Ask for God's peace to fill you so that instead of reacting and allowing the stress to control you, you can respond with God's peace and seize the day.

Training Your Children

Taffi L. Dollar

As for God, his way is perfect;
the word of the LORD is flawless.
He is a shield
for all who take refuge in him.

—2 Samuel 22:31

Secular society has a system for raising children, and so does God. But which produces positive, long-lasting results? There's no doubt about it, parenting according to *biblical* principles has proven to be the most effective. God gave us His Word, so we can make it the final authority in the way we raise our children. Despite the opinions of psychologists, friends, and relatives, the Bible *must* have the last word.

It admonishes us to "rear them [tenderly] in the *training* and discipline and the counsel and admonition of the Lord" (Eph. 6:4 AMP, italics mine). In other words, apply the Word when training your kids, regardless of the situation.

When we train our children God's way, it pleases Him and compels Him to overwhelm our households with His goodness. Training and teaching are different. *Teaching* involves the giving of information, while *training* involves making your children do what you teach them. You're molding their character through exercise and regimentation.

A football coach does not draw plays on a chalkboard and expect his players to automatically execute them at game time. The coach has to train his team over and over until they know how to run those plays proficiently, and he won't quit until they do.

Never forget that God's system for discipline and correction is based on *love,* and love conquers all![58]

make **your** day count

In what area do you feel your children need the most training? Table manners? Courtesy? Grooming? Instead of trying to tackle too many areas at once, choose the one you feel strongest about, discuss it with your children today, then work on it consistently for a period of time until it becomes a habit.

Confidence Builds Intimacy in Marriage

Brenda Timberlake-White

A wife of noble character who can find? She is worth far more than rubies. Her husband has full confidence in her.
—Proverbs 31:10–11

In order for a marriage relationship to be truly intimate, the husband and wife must have confidence in one another. You have confidence in Jesus because over time you have developed a closeness with Him. You know He will keep His Word and that you can trust Him. You can tell Him your most personal secrets. He will never betray you.

In the same way, marriage partners develop confidence in one another by sharing and truly getting to know one another. This takes time, but the effort is worth it. A special closeness develops where no one knows more about you than your mate and you about him. You know each other's strengths and weaknesses, and all secrets are kept safe between you. There is no reason to hold back, because friends look for ways to create security.

Yet often husbands are not intimate with their wives because they know that what they share will be repeated to someone else. Proverbs 16:28 NKJV calls this type of woman a "whisperer," and she separates best friends—even herself from her mate. Instead of nurturing confidence, a wall of distrust is built; and where there is no confidence, fear, complaints, and murmuring will come forth.

Be a person of your word. Build confidence in one another. The result will be the sweet reward of intimacy.[59]

make **your** day count

Examine your heart today. Is your husband able to have total confidence in you? If there are areas that need adjustment, take them to God in prayer and make the necessary changes.

time **saving** tips

Training Your Children to Write Thank-You Notes

Betsy Williams

Training your children to write thank-you notes is a skill that will serve them well throughout their lives. It is a way to train your youngsters in the art of courtesy and graciousness. Doesn't it bless you to receive a note of thanks from others?

Have the kids make their own thank-you notes. You can purchase card stock at any office supply store in a variety of colors. Cut the sheets in half, either lengthwise or across the width. Fold each strip in half. Office supply stores also sell envelopes that fit this size of card.

Give the kids markers, glue, glitter, sequins, construction paper, stickers, and stencils; and let them "go-to-town"decorating! Cutting around the open sides of the cards with crazy scissors adds a unique touch. Fancy hole punches from scrapbook stores work great too.

If your children are old enough to write a brief note of thanks inside, have them do so. If they can only write their names, you write the note and let your children sign the cards. Who wouldn't treasure receiving such a special note!

Evelyn's Shortbread Cookies[60]

Evelyn Roberts

1 lb. butter (room temperature)
1 cup powdered sugar (firmly pressed)
1 tsp. salt
1 tsp. vanilla
5 cups flour

Whip butter with a beater until completely creamed.

Mix butter and sugar until creamy.

Add salt and vanilla.

Add flour slowly. Will need to blend with hands by fifth cup.

Use 1 cup flour to roll out ½ inch thin and use flour to keep
dough together.

Roll out and cut with round cutter on top of glass—well-
floured. (They fall apart easily—even after cooked.)

Bake at 350° on ungreased cookie sheet 35 to 45 minutes until
light brown on top.

Breakthrough!

Lindsay Roberts

A merry heart does good, like a medicine,
but a broken spirit dries the bones.
—Proverbs 17:22 NKJV

When my daughter Olivia was a young fifty-pound girl, she accidentally ate some food I had intended to throw out. Within an hour, she was vomiting uncontrollably, passing blood. In the emergency room they confirmed she had food poisoning from the deadly E-coli bacteria.

Guilt hit me like I had never known before. I was absolutely bombarded with terrifying thoughts like, *This is so much your fault that you ought to just die with her.* On the outside I was praying, but on the inside, I was stabbing myself to death, knowing I could have prevented it.

Spending many days in the hospital, I felt like I couldn't breathe and needed to get out and change the atmosphere. I decided to go to Target to buy Olivia a Barbie she had been wanting. Right in the aisle, I began to feel my guts ripping out. I was totally overcome with agony. I cried out to God, "You have to take this from me."

Seemingly out of nowhere, the Barbie representative showed up and began telling me about these incredibly expensive collector Barbies, totally diverting my attention. But actually, the Holy Spirit was setting me up.

I thought, *A Barbie that costs more than your groceries?* for no reason, something about it hit me, and I began laughing hysterically right in front of the Barbie rep. And believe me, I was not trying to be rude. She was very kind. To make a long story short, the laughter broke the oppression! I was released and knew Olivia was okay. When I returned to the hospital, she was up and out of bed. Victory![61]

make **your** day count

No matter what happens today, God can put you over. Cry out to Him if you feel overcome with negative thoughts and feelings. Find Bible verses about joy and assurance. Allow God's supernatural joy to break through.

The Power of a Mother's Prayer

Marilyn Hickey

The seed of the righteous shall be delivered.
—Proverbs 11:21 KJV

I knew a woman whose son had been classified by the police as a hopeless, habitual criminal. The woman meditated on and prayed the above verse over her son. She even proclaimed by faith, "I know God is going to save my son. He will preach in this church." She focused all her attention on God's *transforming power.*

One night, she felt an unusual burden to pray in the Spirit for her son. An hour later, he called her long distance, asking what she had been doing earlier. He said a man to whom he'd sold some bad drugs had come to his apartment, beaten him to a pulp, then pulled out a gun, intending to shoot him. The man tried to pull the trigger, but couldn't bend his finger! Finally, he threw the gun down and ran out, declaring, "Your mother is doing something to stop me from pulling this trigger!"

Needless to say, the son received Jesus as his Lord and was filled with the Holy Spirit shortly thereafter. He attended Bible school and was later a guest speaker at his mother's church, just as his mother had declared.

You children *can* be transformed! Whether they are grown and living a life of sin or still at home under your covering, the transforming power of God's Word is available to help them.[62]

make **your** day count

Find a Bible promise that pertains to an area of concern you have toward your children. Begin stating that promise as fact, and stand your ground in prayer. Your prayers avail much in the lives of your children.

Healed of Cancer

Dodie Osteen

He sent forth his word and healed them;
he rescued them from the grave.
—Psalm 107:20

On December 10, 1981, I was diagnosed with metastatic cancer of the liver. I was told I only had a few weeks to live, even if I pursued treatment.

As the head of our house, my husband, John Osteen, anointed me with oil. Together we took authority over any disease and cancerous cells in my body. (Mark 16:17–18.) That was on December 11, 1981, the day I believe my healing began.

In spite of every discouraging symptom and the enormous fear that would come against me, my heart knew that God's Word promised healing and His Word could not lie. If I had not had confidence in that, I would have died. But day by day, I clung to my Bible and its healing promises. The Word became my life, and it healed me.

The Word of God is extremely important to people who are fighting a battle for their health, because often it's the only hope they have. I am so thankful to be alive today and to be able to bring you a message of hope! You can win the battle against sickness. I did not get healed because I am special. I was healed because I dared to take God at His

Word. You can do that too. And what God did for me, He'll also do for you.[63]

make **your** day count

Are you or is someone you know facing illness today? Read the many healing Scriptures found in the Bible. Then dare to take God at His Word, and receive the healing that Jesus has provided for you.

time **saving** tips

Fitness on the Go

Betsy Williams

Always consult your doctor first, but consider these easy-to-incorporate fitness tips:

Take the stairs.

Take the dog for a walk.

Park away from the door in parking lots.

Walk up the escalator.

Hold in your stomach at stop lights, fifteen seconds for each rep.

Swing with your kids at the park.

Take a walk with your family around the neighborhood.

Ride a stationary bike while watching your favorite TV program.

Dance!

Do step exercises while dinner cooks.

Vacuum the house.

Spinach Squares[64]

Dodie Osteen

¼ cup butter or margarine

3 large eggs, beaten

1 cup flour

1 cup milk

½ tsp. salt

1 tsp. baking powder

1 lb. Monterey Jack cheese, grated

2 10-oz. pkgs. frozen chopped spinach, thawed and squeezed dry

Preheat over to 350°.

In a 9- x 13-inch baking dish, melt butter.

Blend together the eggs, flour, milk, salt, and baking powder.

Add cheese and spinach, stirring well.

Spread the mixture in the baking dish and bake for 35 minutes.

Cool 30 minutes before cutting into squares.

Note: these squares freeze well.

A Blueprint That Works

Lindsay Roberts

Be doers of the word, and not hearers only.
—James 1:22 NKJV

In math we learn that two plus two equals four. And every time we add those numbers, the result is the same. However, if we change the *plus* to a *minus*, we destroy the equation, and the answer becomes quite different.

God has given us a plan and a purpose—plus a specific procedure to fulfill that plan. It's called the Word of God. As we pour ourselves into Scripture, we soon begin to understand that God's blueprint will work again and again.

There are two reasons we can trust what our heavenly Father declares:

1. God's Word is truth. "God is not a man, that he should lie" (Num. 23:19 KJV).

2. God's Word never changes. God declared, "I am the LORD, I change not" (Mal. 3:6 KJV).

You were not created to be perpetually stressed, frustrated, and upset. That is not God's desire. He sees you winning in life. Deuteronomy 28:13 says, "The LORD will make you the head, not the tail. If you pay attention to the commands of the LORD your God that I give you this day and carefully follow them, you will always be at the top, never at the bottom."

It's a lot like having a drawer full of makeup. What a difference it makes when you actually apply it. God's Word is just the same.[65]

make **your** day count

Instead of being overtaken by stress, find a Scripture on God's peace and meditate on it today. For example, you could ponder Philippians 4:6–7 and pray, "Thank You God for Your peace that passes my understanding. Help me walk in Your peace, so I won't worry today."

Disciplining Your Children With Love

Patricia Salem

Don't make your children angry by the way you treat them. Rather, bring them up with the discipline and instruction approved by the Lord.
—Ephesians 6:4 NLT

If you want to be a good parent, look at how our heavenly Father parents us, His children. He gently guides and leads us with loving kindness, tender mercies, and correction. Discipline as taught in the Scriptures means to make a disciple out of a child by training. A loving parent administers discipline promptly and then works quickly to restore fellowship with the child.

When my children would misbehave, I would send them to their rooms to think about what they had done. When they could come out, I'd ask them to tell me what they had done wrong and what they thought the punishment should be. This kind of discipline helped them take responsibility for what they had done wrong and helped them know how they needed to act in the future.

It also gave me time to release any frustration or anger I might have felt. No matter what method you choose to train your children, don't punish a child when you are angry or fearful of what you might say, because words can't be taken back.

Our role as parents is the same as that of the Good Shepherd toward His sheep. If we learn how our loving heavenly Father parents us, we can raise our children so that they will grow up to be loving and responsible.[66]

make **your** day count

Make it a point to incorporate these ideas into disciplining your children today. Also, think about how your heavenly Father parents you with such great love. He disciplines you then forgives you quickly, so you can get back on track.

Knowing God

Gloria Copeland

The Son of God has come and has given us understanding,
so that we may know him who is true.

—1 John 5:20

If you want to know God, you will have to spend time with Him, talking to Him and communing with Him. That's living contact. It's listening to Him and obeying what you hear and what you find in God's Word. Learning to live in the place where God can talk to you at any moment is the secret to living an overcoming life.

To know Him should be the number-one priority in every Christian's life. It is the key that opens every spiritual door. Daily communion with God—being intimate with Him—strengthens you and undergirds your faith. It's the way love works. A living connection with God produces the anointing that enables you to lay hold of all the wonderful things God has provided for us through Jesus Christ.

What you will have in your life tomorrow is determined by what is in your heart today. So, when you daily fill your heart with the Word and the voice of God, you will abide in Him. As you feast your heart on His promises and His presence, then your future will be one of joy and prosperity, healing and health. Instead of chasing after the blessings of

God, you'll find they're chasing you and overtaking you at every turn! Understanding this has changed my life forever.[67]

make **your** day count

Be aware that God is with you every minute today. Talk to Him about the decisions you have to make. Receive His peace and let it envelop you if you feel yourself getting stressed out. Talk to Him like you would your best friend, and then listen to what He has to say to you.

Give Them to God

Evelyn Roberts

I know whom I have believed, and am convinced that he is
able to guard what I have entrusted to him for that day.
—2 Timothy 1:12

When our children were born, we dedicated them to the Lord. I thought I had really committed them to God until Ronnie, our oldest son, quit college to join the army. I wanted him to finish college, which he did later, but he wanted to try something on his own. We were both frustrated. I didn't realize it at the time, but I was trying to help the Lord plan Ronnie's life.

One day I got down on my knees and really gave Ronnie to the Lord. I said, "Lord, I've tried to hold on to my children even after I gave them to You when they were born. But now I really commit them—especially Ronnie—to You. I will never again put my hand on their lives. They are in Your care." With that prayer the burden lifted, and I experienced a wonderful release.

Life is filled with inevitable adjustments. And one of the greatest of these is giving up our hold on our children—to let them go out and face life on their own, to let them experience their own pain and their own joy. This process of relinquishment actually begins soon after they are born, and it isn't easy. But God is faithful, and we can commit them to His care, knowing He loves them even more than we do.[68]

make **your** day count

Name each of your children and present him or her to God in prayer. Commit your children, their decisions, their futures, and everything about them to God's loving care. Then rest in His loving arms.

time **saving** tips

Handmade Wrapping Paper and Gift Bags

Betsy Williams

Let the kids make their own wrapping paper. Buy a roll of brown paper used to wrap boxes for shipping or a roll of white butcher paper. Give the kids markers, stencils, and paints, which they can use to decorate. Sponge paints work great; you can purchase the assorted shaped sponges and tempera paint at craft stores. They can make themed wrapping paper for Valentine's Day, Christmas, and birthdays. The choices are endless!

The kids can also make their own party-favor bags for their birthday parties. White lunch sacks work great, but for a boys' party, you might prefer brown lunch sacks. First, write the names of each recipient on the bags. Then your kids can decorate the bags. When they are done, fold over the tops of the bags about two inches. Use a hole- punch to make two holes side by side about an inch apart and an inch from the top of the fold. Thread the holes with colorful curling ribbons and tie. These also work well in lieu of the handled gift bags you can buy in stores.

Lindsay's Frozen Grapes[69]

Wash grapes. While they are still wet, roll them in white sugar or a natural sugar substitute.

Place toothpick straight up in each one. Freeze and serve frozen.

Be aware that grapes are high in sugar. It's a natural fruit sugar, but it's still sugar.

My girls love to eat these frozen grapes. You can serve them frozen in chicken salad or fresh lettuce salads. The grapes thaw quickly and add a cold twist to your salads.

Four Ingredients for Godly Discipline

Taffi L. Dollar

Discipline your son, and he will give you peace;
he will bring delight to your soul.

—Proverbs 29:17

The following are some practical ways to train your children according to God's system.

- Establish specific, reasonable rules. Make sure they are written down and clearly understood.

- When your children break the rules, deal with it *immediately,* if possible. Make sure they understand what they did to displease you, and let them know God's attitude concerning their behavior by showing them what the Bible says.

- If you truly love your children, you will spank them when they become unruly and need correction. The rod should not be used to invoke fear or to injure your child. The objective is to deliver the message that disobedience will not be tolerated. Take time to cool down before you spank your child. Then you will be in a position to clearly communicate your displeasure with their behavior in a loving manner.

- Prayer should follow spanking. This is a time of restoration—a time for your children to realize that you still love them. Both of you should express your love for one another and use some form of affection.

You are never alone, even if you're a single parent having to raise your kids by yourself. The Word of God is the tool you need to succeed in being a good parent.[70]

make **your** day count

Are your house rules written down and clearly understood by each member of the family? If not, take time to write them down, then hold a brief family meeting to communicate your expectations. Perhaps you could also share Scriptures that talk about ways that God blesses obedience.

A Mother's Faith

Marilyn Hickey

Do not throw away your confidence;
it will be richly rewarded.
—Hebrews 10:35

There is something unique about a mother's faith. It allows us to give our children the benefit of the doubt even in bad situations. The Syrophenician mother certainly stretched out in faith on behalf of her hurting daughter.

"A woman of Canaan...cried unto [Jesus], saying, Have mercy on me...; my daughter is grievously vexed with a devil.... But he answered and said, It is not meet to take the children's bread, and to cast it to dogs. And she said, Truth, Lord: yet the dogs eat of the crumbs which fall from their masters' table. Then Jesus answered and said unto her, O woman, great is thy faith: be it unto thee even as thou wilt. And her daughter was made whole from that very hour" (Matt. 15:22,26–28 KJV).

Your children may not be this troubled, but all children need that same kind of spiritual tenacity exerted on their behalf. Put your faith in God's Word. Although your children may be involved in ungodly lifestyles, don't let go of God's transforming power. Remember the Prodigal Son? The Bible says, "He came to himself," (Luke 15:17 KJV). Suddenly his eyes were opened and he saw things from the perspective of

God's Word rather than the world. Your wayward children will do the same. One day, they will hear the Holy Spirit speaking to their hearts and respond.[71]

make **your** day count

Are all of your children living for God? If not, pray that God will open their eyes, so they will "come to themselves" as the Prodigal Son did. Pray for God's power to transform their lives, and don't give up! God is at work.

When Someone You Love Is Ill

Dee Simmons

These three remain: faith, hope and love.
But the greatest of these is love.

—1 Corinthians 13:13

Without any doubt, love helps us heal. Doctors observe the potent effects of the connection between love and medicine. I believe love is as necessary to healing as any amount of clinical expertise, state-of-the-art treatments, or the newest drugs or surgical techniques. When we are sick and scared, we need love and lots of it.

So what can you do to express your love to someone who is fighting a life-threatening illness? Remember:

- Your love is needed and essential.

- You are a part of the patient's healing process.

- Follow your heart.

- Be willing to schedule time to do the small tasks that mean so much, and do them with great love.

- Gentleness and quiet companionship are like a soothing balm.

- Love boldly. Do not fear rejection.

- Write one- or two-sentence love notes to hide in books, drawers, or bathrobe pockets for your loved one to discover.

- Read aloud. Choose beautiful, short, inspiring passages.

- Smile often. Gently touch your loved one's skin, hold his hand, smooth her hair. Stay connected.

- Remember: God is love, so pray for them constantly and let them know it.

Walking through a serious illness with someone is not easy, but that is when the person needs you the most. Your love can make a difference.[72]

make **your** day count

Whether you know someone with a serious health concern
or you see someone who is just having a rough day,
take the opportunity to express your love today.

time **saving** tips

Beauty Tips[73]

Dee Simmons

I remember my mother always saying to me when I was growing up, "You have to get your beauty sleep." And she was right! When I've had eight hours of sleep, I really do look better.

I believe good nutrition and drinking enough water are also important in helping to have younger-looking skin. Here is a simple formula that I use to determine the amount of water I need to drink: I divide my weight in half and drink that amount of water in ounces each day. For instance, 150 pounds divided by 2 equals 75 ounces of water a day.

Chocolate No-Bake Cookies[74]

2 cups sugar
$\frac{1}{2}$ cup milk
4 Tbsp. dry cocoa mix
$\frac{1}{2}$ tsp. salt
1 stick butter ($\frac{1}{2}$ cup)
$\frac{1}{4}$–$\frac{1}{2}$ cup peanut butter (optional)
2 tsp. vanilla
3 cups uncooked quick cooking oats

Mix sugar, milk, cocoa, salt, and butter; and bring to highest boil.

Boil one minute and remove from heat.

Add peanut butter, vanilla, and dry oats. Mix well.

Drop by teaspoonfuls onto waxed paper.

When God Says "Pssst!"

Gloria Copeland

Those of Ephraim shall be like a mighty man,
And their heart shall rejoice as if with wine.
Yes, their children shall see it and be glad;
Their heart shall rejoice in the LORD.
I will whistle for them and gather them,
For I will redeem them.

—Zechariah 10:7–8 NKJV

Once when Ken and I were in Australia, thoughts of our son, John, flooded my heart. John was a teenager at the time—all boy. He rode everything with wheels, and it seemed he was always turning something over. I knew how much the devil would like to sneak in and steal John's life, and I was concerned that his misadventures could provide the opportunity to do it. But the Holy Spirit spoke to Ken and said, *My mercy hovers over John.* As I've prayed for John throughout the years, that wonderful word from God has often risen up and reminded me that John's life is secure.

You may not even know where your children are right now. But the text verse says that when you rejoice in the Lord, your children will see it and turn. God will signal for them: *Pssst!* And they'll come running. It doesn't matter what kind of wickedness that child has fallen into, God can still reach him. Don't ever give up. Dig into God's Word and dig out the promises He's given you for your children.

Your covenant with God covers your children, so rejoice! One day your boy or your girl will be going about his or her business, when suddenly—*Pssst!*—they'll hear the voice of God and come running. You can count on it.[75]

make **your** day count

God's mercy hovers over your children. Whenever you think of them today, rejoice, even if the situation looks bad. Your praise is a sign of your faith, and as you trust God to reach your children, the door will be open for Him to get their attention and bring them back to Him.

From Stressing to Blessing

Lindsay Roberts

Count it all joy when ye fall into divers temptations;
knowing this, that the trying of your faith worketh
patience. But let patience have her perfect work,
that ye may be perfect and entire, wanting nothing.
—James 1:2–5 KJV

Note the two key words *knowing this* above. The joy is not in falling. The joy is in *knowing this*, that the trying of our faith works patience in us.

The word *patience* means "hopeful endurance, constancy, continuance, waiting, calm endurance of hardness, capacity, provocation of pain, tolerance, perseverance, forbearance, diligence, tenacity, doggedness, self-possessed waiting."

What an exciting plan to move from *stressing* to *blessing*. Instead of failing, the Bible tells us we can be *complete, perfect, made whole,* and *wanting nothing.* How does it happen? Through the joy of *knowing.*

What we know is that God has a master plan that "all things work together for good to them that love God, to them who are the called according to his purpose" (Rom. 8:28 KJV). It doesn't say that all things *are* good, but it does say all things work together *for* good. For whom? For those who love the Lord and are called according to His purpose. God is working things out *for our good,* and that's not just *a* master plan—it's *the* Master's plan. It's God's blueprint for our lives.[76]

make **your** day count

Take comfort in the fact that no matter what you face today, God can work it out for your good. Invite Him to be in charge of your day, and thank Him for His involvement in your life.

Mark Your Children for God

Marilyn Hickey

*[Hannah said], "O LORD Almighty, if you will only look
upon your servant's misery and remember me, and not
forget your servant but give her a son, then I will give him
to the LORD for all the days of his life."*

—1 Samuel 1:11

While earthly riches pass away, the things you invest in
your children will not. Your children can serve God on this
earth long after you have left; then they can join you in eternity with Jesus Christ. However, you must "mark" your children (point them to God and parent them with a godly
perspective), declaring them "off limits" to Satan.

Hannah marked Samuel before conception. Keeping her
promise to God that she would give the child to the Lord,
she sent him to live with the priest Eli at the temple in a
negative, ungodly environment. Your children also live in
an ungodly world, but they need not be affected by it. If
you mark them for God, they will hear God's voice despite
their surroundings.

When Pharaoh marked Jewish children for death, Moses'
parents hid him and "marked" (circumcised) him for God—
before placing him in an ark on the Nile. Moses was marked
to deliver God's people from bondage.

If you think that just because you are a Christian, your children will be Christians, think again. Only by following God's divine instructions for marking your children can you expect divine results.

- Discipline your children.

- Set the example.

- Teach them to hide God's Word in their hearts.

- Nurture a healthy self-image in your children.

- Be quick to forgive; love unconditionally.[77]

make **your** day count

Pray for your children and commit them and their lives to God to be used for His service. Evaluate the five principles above and make any adjustments that are needed. Pick one area to work on today.

Making a Happy Home

Pat Harrison

He must manage his own family well.

—1 Timothy 3:4

I know it isn't easy to keep your home in order. Frequently both parents work, and the kids are involved in many extracurricular activities. This often means that no one ever eats together. All the family members come in late from their activities, retreat to their rooms, and go to bed. That isn't a home; it's a house being used as a way station.

Do everything within your power to create a happy home life where family members regularly enjoy times of fellowship and fun together. My children were involved in after-school activities. However, I never allowed them to get so involved that we could not have a home life. The tendency today is for parents to think that the more activities their children can be involved in, the better their lives will be. That is not necessarily true. A strong family is more important than any football game, cheerleading practice, or dance lesson.

If possible, dinnertime should be reserved as family time. It blesses me when my children say that some of their best memories of home are the times we sat around the dinner table having a good time as a family, laughing and talking about the things that happened during the day. These precious times of enjoying each other's company strengthened our family unit, and I believe they will do the same for you.[78]

make **your** day count

If at all possible, plan for your family to eat dinner together tonight, making it a family time. Ask open-ended questions of your other family members, and show a genuine interest in their answers.

time **saving** tips

Laundry Made Simple

When it comes to laundry, it is often difficult to tell whose socks are whose. Choose a different color of thread for each family member and sew a few stitches in the toes of each sock. When the socks are clean, have each child pull out his or her color-coordinated pairs of socks. This works on underwear too.

You can apply this same principle to bath towels as well. Purchase one set of bath towels for each child, each child having his or her own color. For example Julie might want pink towels and Jackson likes blue. For fun, give the kids assorted buttons, ribbon, sequins, and other ornamentation to decorate the edge of their towels. When the towels have been washed, each child can pull out his or her own clean towels to fold and put away. And if someone happens to leave a wet towel on the floor? Well, you'll know who to summon to pick it up!

Easy "Creamy" Broccoli Soup

Betsy Williams

This soup gives the appearance of being creamy, although it has
  no cream or milk in it.

1 ½ lbs. broccoli, stemmed and chopped
3 cups chicken broth
2 medium-sized green onions, cut in two-inch lengths
1 stalk celery, strings removed and chopped
½ tsp. salt

Combine all ingredients in medium saucepan.

Cover and cook over medium-low heat until broccoli is tender,
  about 7 minutes.

Puree in blender in batches until smooth, and serve.

God's Word on Successful Parenting

Taffi L. Dollar

As the rain and the snow come down from heaven, and do not return to it without watering the earth and making it bud and flourish, so that it yields seed for the sower and bread for the eater, so is my word that goes out from my mouth: It will not return to me empty, but will accomplish what I desire and achieve the purpose for which I sent it.

—Isaiah 55:10–11

As you meditate on the Word of God daily, your faith in the promises of God is built up. When those Scriptures become more real to you than what you see with your physical eyes, that is when those promises will come to pass. The following is a prayer you can pray aloud every day to see a difference in your relationships with your children.

Lord, I thank You for my children. I recognize that they are a heritage and a reward. You have given them to me as an assignment, and I purpose in my heart to help them discover their calling. I will build my children up and let them know that they can do all things through Christ. I thank You for the wisdom and knowledge that You have given me to impart to them, knowing that it will produce an abundant harvest in their lives and mine. Help me to always chastise my children in love so that they won't despise correction, but will recognize it as an act of Your love for them. Help me to restore and honor my kids after I correct them, so I can point them toward repentance. Help me to display consistency, discipline, and love daily. As I train my children in the principles of the Word, I ask You to fulfill Your will for their lives. In Jesus' name, amen.[79]

make **your** day count

Look up the following verses from which this prayer is taken and meditate on how they apply to your children: Psalm 127:3, Philippians 4:13, Proverbs 23:24, and Proverbs 3:11.

Never, Never Give Up

Patricia Salem

Let us not get tired of doing what is right,
for after a while we will reap a harvest of
blessing if we don't get discouraged and give up.
—Galatians 6:9 TLB

My son Harry was ten when his father died of leukemia. One day Harry wanted to learn how to play football because he had entered a punt, pass, and kick competition.

"Mom," he told me, "I don't know how to kick the football off a tee because I don't have one, and I have never had anyone show me how."

I knew nothing about football, but God will always make a way if you trust Him. I went out and bought a leather football, a kicking tee, and a book on how to play. I didn't have any idea about how to kick a football, but I was determined to teach Harry.

Out in the yard, I set the football on the tee, backed up, took a running start, and kicked the stuffing out of that football. Unfortunately, I kicked the stuffing out of my foot too! I broke several blood vessels and wound up with the worst swollen, black-and-blue mess you've ever seen.

As Harry helped me inside, he said, "Well, that's that. I'll never learn how to kick a football."

But if I've learned one thing through losing my husband and rearing our three children, it's never, never give up! Take one day at a time, and if you fail at something one day, try harder the next.

"Don't think this is going to stop us," I told Harry. "Tomorrow I'll wear socks!"[80]

make **your** day count

What obstacle are you facing today?
No matter what it is, with God, there's always a way.
Commit that thing to God and get out there and play ball.

Living From Your Spirit

Lindsay Roberts

Bless the LORD, O my soul: and all that is
within me, bless his holy name. Bless the LORD,
O my soul, and forget not all his benefits.
—Psalm 103:1–2 KJV

To enjoy a life full of God's blessing, we must put our spirits first, our souls second (mind, will, and emotions), and our bodies last. But sometimes we let our souls take control and the spiritual part of us just gets dragged along. There are five things we can do to keep the spiritual part of us in charge.

1. Bless the Lord in all you do. Pay close attention to what you watch, hear, say, and think. Too many negative influences will drag you down.

2. Feed your soul. We feed our bodies the right kind of food, so they'll function properly, and our souls are no different. Just like your stomach, your soul is going to get used to whatever you feed it. Feed it God's Word, and You will begin to crave it.

3. Use the sword of God's Word to cut the garbage out. You're going to have all kinds of thoughts, and it's up to you to process them. When you hear something that doesn't agree with God's Word, cut it out.

4. Shut the back door. The back door is that thing that you don't want to give up or yield to God. But if you commit it to Him, He will separate that thing from you, so that only the pure remains.

5. Expect a miracle.[81]

make **your** day count

Feed your soul some of God's good Word today. When negative thoughts try to take over your thinking, reflect on a Bible passage to counteract that thought. Then your spirit will be leading your soul.

time **saving** tips

Adding Laughter to Your Life[82]

Laughter can benefit us in many ways. It releases endorphins, natural chemicals in the body that create a feeling of pleasure and have a pain-relieving effect. It relieves stress and helps us keep things in perspective. It unites us to others. It activates the chemistry of the will to live and increases our capacity to fight disease. Perhaps best of all, it simply makes us feel better and enjoy life more. Laughter is best when shared with others.

Here are some tips to add laughter and humor to your everyday life:

 Hang around funny friends.

 See the world through your children's eyes.

Look for the absurd, silly, incongruous activities that go on around you each day.

 Take a five- to ten-minute humor break each day. Read jokes and comic strips.

Rent comedy videos or go to see a funny movie.

 If you hear a joke you really like, write it down or tell it to someone else to help you remember it.

 Read funny cards in the grocery store or card shop.

Seven Layer Cookies[83]

$^1\!/_2$ cup butter (1 stick)

1 pkg. graham crackers, crushed

1 cup coconut, shredded

1 cup walnuts, chopped

6 oz. chocolate chips

6 oz. butterscotch chips

6 oz. sweetened condensed milk

Melt butter in a cookie pan.

Sprinkle graham cracker crumbs in the butter first.

Then sprinkle coconut, chocolate chips, and butterscotch chips over the crumbs.

Pour the sweetened condensed milk over all and sprinkle the nuts on top.

Bake at 350° for 30–35 minutes.

Cut into squares.

Build Deeply in Their Lives

Evelyn Roberts

Train the younger women to love their husbands and
children, to be self-controlled and pure, to be busy
at home, to be kind, and to be subject to their husbands,
so that no one will malign the word of God.

—Titus 2:4–5

My heart goes out to parents who have so many demands made on their time. I always encourage them to set aside a specific time for their family and not permit anything to interfere with it. Some say, "But people will never understand. I've promised to do this and that."

"You're not responsible for people who don't understand you," I remind them. "You are responsible to God for the rearing and motivation of your children."

I could have been doing something for someone or speaking to a group every day my children were growing up, but I refused to let anything keep me from the time that belonged to them. While my husband traveled in the ministry, I divided my time between him and the children because I felt both needed me, and that's where I belonged.

I believe we should learn from Jesus and build deeply in the lives of our family members. Jesus loved everyone, but He concentrated on twelve men. By building deeply in the lives of those few, Jesus planted seeds of the continuation of His ministry.

As often as possible, set aside time to be with your family—to read the Bible, pray, or just enjoy being together. This will deepen your love for one another. The greatest gift you can give your children is yourself.[84]

make **your** day count

In what way can you give yourself to your children today?
Set aside some time, even if it is only fifteen minutes,
and give them your undivided attention.

More Than a New Year's Resolution

Marty Copeland

[Jesus said], "If the Son sets you free,
you will be free indeed."
—John 8:36

A New Year's resolution promises gain, but lacks the substance to produce it. Any resolution that tries to bring about a transformation by fleshly effort instead of by the power of God sets you up for failure. True change and total victory occur only when we exercise our faith in the transforming power of God.

For over half my life, I was in bondage to overeating. I was obsessed with diets and exercise. I lost close to a total of seven hundred pounds through years of gaining then losing weight. Today, I'm totally, 100 percent free and experiencing the joy that comes with that freedom.

In theory, resolutions *sound* good, but they are just carnal methods that keep us frustrated and failing until finally we lose all hope of ever being free. There is a way out, however. You will need to make a quality decision to put your hope and faith in God.

As you continue in God's Word, trusting Him to conform you to the image of His Son, the burden-removing, yoke-destroying power of Jesus the Anointed One and His anointing will set you free from the bondage of weight and the weight of bondage. (Isa. 10:27.) You can confidently put your hope and trust in Him because when the Son makes you free, you are free indeed![85]

make **your** day count

Today, submit any areas of bondage to the Lord and
His yoke-destroying anointing. Ask Him to help you change
the things you can, then trust that He is transforming you even
when you don't see change. The Son will set you free!

You Hold the Key

Marilyn Hickey

The prayer of a righteous man is powerful and effective.
—James 5:16

Your faith in God's transforming power will determine the course of your child's life. Moses' mother was Jochebed. Pharaoh ordered all the newborn male Hebrews murdered, but Jochebed trusted God. She had a mother's faith for her baby. She hid him, then put him in an ark and floated him down a river to Pharaoh's daughter who was bathing downstream. She named him Moses and raised him as her own.

Because of his mother's faith, Moses' life was spared; he received an excellent education and had the best of everything. After some life-changing learning experiences, he answered the call of God to deliver the children of Israel from Pharaoh's bondage in Egypt. This included the parting of the Red Sea!

Looking back on the circumstances surrounding Moses' birth, would you have foreseen all of this in his future? I doubt it; but God's transforming power turned Moses' life around.

Maybe your decisions haven't always served God and you've made some mistakes in raising your children. The good news is that, regardless of their beginnings, God has plans for them—they may be future deliverers in the body of

Christ. Stop feeling guilty about mistakes you may have made. Seek God and ask for forgiveness. Then ask your children to forgive you and stand on God's Word—the transforming power for their lives.[86]

make **your** day count

Is guilt weighing you down? Go to God with it and in its place receive His love and forgiveness. If you need to make things right with your children, do so today. Then trust God to watch over them and lead them to their destiny.

You Are a Whosoever

Lindsay Roberts

God so loved the world, that he gave his only
begotten Son, that whosoever believeth in him
should not perish, but have everlasting life.

—John 3:16 KJV

If you've never given your heart to Jesus, then it's time to go to the Cross and surrender *all* to Him. Remember, God gave His only begotten Son that *whosoever* believes in Him would not perish—*and whosoever includes you!*

Don't ever let anybody tell you that God's salvation doesn't include you, because every translation of the Bible I've ever read says that it includes *anyone* who comes to Him. God wrote *whosoever* because He meant to say *whosoever.* You can have a fresh, new start if you'll pray this prayer out loud:

Father God, I come to the Cross, and I surrender all. I received Your Son, Jesus Christ, as my Lord and Savior. Forgive me of my sins. Cleanse me, and give me a new life. This is my new beginning. This is my fresh chance. In Jesus' name it's starting-over time for me. Old things have passed away and all things have become new. (2 Cor. 5:17.) In Jesus' name, amen.

If you prayed that prayer and meant it from your heart, all the old mistakes from the past are now forgiven. All the failures, all the sins, are washed away and covered by the blood of Jesus. You're a new creature in Christ, *and now it's time for you to become everything God has called you to be!*[87]

make **your** day count

If you have never made Jesus Christ Lord of your life, do it today! This day could count more than any other day of your life on earth. Don't put it off. You are one of the whosoevers God wants to spend eternity with.

time **saving** tips

Organizing Recipes

To organize recipes you clip out of magazines, put them in a small photo album that you can pick up at the dollar store.

These inexpensive photo albums are also the right size to hold 3 x 5 inch cards, so you could write all your favorite recipes on index cards and store them in this one handy book.

If you prefer using a card file, laminate all of your favorite recipes to keep them from getting soiled.

Volcano Cupcakes

Cleo Justus

1 box chocolate cake mix
Paper cupcake holders
Large marshmallows
Chopped nuts

Prepare cake batter as directed on package.

Place 1 paper cupcake holder in each section of muffin pan.

Fill each paper cup ½ full of cake batter.

Add one marshmallow and push down to bottom of cup.

Add more batter to make paper cup ¾ full and sprinkle with chopped nuts.

Bake as directed on package.

These are very good, and each one will look different on top.
No need to add frosting, unless you just want to.

What's Influencing Your Children?

Taffi L. Dollar

I will walk in my house with blameless heart.
I will set before my eyes no vile thing.

—Psalm 101:2–3

In these last days, deception will increase—that's a guarantee. Therefore, be mindful of what your children are exposed to. You don't want them to grow up confused about life and the life that God wants them to live. There are many, many evil and deceptive influences that would try to confuse and seduce young people. (Eph. 4:14.)

I encourage you to discuss the content of movies, video games, sitcoms, magazines, and comic books with your children. Rather than change the channel when something questionable comes on TV, talk to your kids about it. Ask them whether or not Jesus would watch or listen to it. The balance, however, is not to allow their young minds to become saturated with ungodliness in an effort to teach them a lesson. Images are seeds.

You may also want to provide alternatives for those things that you ban from your home. Visit your local Christian retail store with your children and purchase CDs,

videos, and magazines that appeal to them. Review the mate-
rial with them so that *together* you can make sound decisions.

As with anything concerning your kids, don't ever com-
promise godly standards and the boundaries you establish.
Protect them in love, and love will help you to balance things
out. Trust God's direction, and your children will become
programmed to live for Him and Him alone![88]

make **your** day count

Sit down and watch the programs your children want to watch today.
Listen to the music they listen to. Give them an opportunity to tell
you why they like those particular things. Then discuss how things
could influence them in a good way or a negative way.

Pray Daily for Your Children

Pat Harrison

God knows how often I pray for you. Day and night I
bring you and your needs in prayer to the one I serve.
—Romans 1:9 TLB

There is nothing more beneficial or powerful you can do for your children than to intercede in prayer for them every day. If they are in school, you should pray against the powers of darkness and negative influences that would try to come against them. Stand your ground in Jesus' name, confident that they are protected because you have asked God for that divine protection in faith.

Do not put off praying for your children until you sense urgency in your spirit. Don't wait until Susie is really acting strange and you are wondering, *Why is she acting that way?* Rely on the Holy Spirit's direction. Sometimes during the day, a thought may come to you about your child. Most people think, *Oh, that's just me; I'm such an overprotective mother,* but many times it is the Holy Spirit prompting you to pray.

Perhaps your child is having a problem in school and God wants you to intervene in prayer on his or her behalf. Help him or her understand what is going on from a spiritual perspective and then deal with the situation. Sit down with your child and read Scriptures that pertain to the situation; then pray about the problem in Jesus' name. This can actually be a time in which you and your child grow closer as you tackle the situation together.[89]

make **your** day count

Each time you think of your children today, say a brief prayer, asking
God to surround them and fill them with His love, joy, and peace.
Take a stand in prayer against the forces of darkness that
would try to harass or steal the peace of your children.

Encourage Yourself in the Lord

Lindsay Roberts

To you, O LORD, I lift up my soul;
in you I trust, O my God.
—Psalm 25:1–2

Not long ago, I was really exhausted and so emotional! I didn't yell at anybody or hurt anyone, but I was being a jerk and having a pity party. The funny thing was, nobody came to that party but me.

According to the verse above, I knew I had to encourage myself to get over the situation that had put me in such a bad frame of mind. I had to lift up my soul—my mind, my will, and my emotions—to God.

Whether it's a personal problem or the world situation that is affecting you, it's not hard to get discouraged. We often call on others to help encourage us, and that's good, but there comes a time when you have to lay all that aside and make a conscious decision to encourage yourself, to lift up your soul to God. What's interesting is that as you lift up your soul to God and begin to praise Him, He jumps on your bandwagon. But He won't begin doing His part— strengthening all aspects of your life and multiplying the harvest of the spiritual seed you've sown—until you begin doing your part, which is to bless Him.

Psalm 22:3 KJV says that God inhabits the praises of His people, so when we begin to praise Him, lifting up our souls, He will start acting on our behalf.[90]

make **your** day count

Make a conscious effort to lift up your soul to God today, praising Him for His goodness and all that He's blessed you with. When you get your eyes off of your problems and onto Him, He will lift you up.

time **saving** tips

Kitchen Tips[91]

To soften a stick of hard cold butter, shred it with a grater.

To extend the life of garlic, store the peeled cloves in salad oil in the refrigerator.

Eggs at room temperature will beat better and provide more volume.

When whipping heavy cream, always use a stainless steel bowl and never an aluminum one. Aluminum will cause the cream to turn grayish and will give it a metallic taste.

Frozen fish can be thawed in cold water, and it will not affect the quality of the fish.

Quick and Easy Tex-Mex Dip

1 8-oz. container sour cream
1 8-oz. package cream cheese
1 package taco seasoning
Salsa
Shredded cheese

Mix first three ingredients well.

After dip has set for a few hours, top with salsa and sprinkle
cheese over all.

Give God to Your Children

Evelyn Roberts

Listen, my son, to your father's instruction
and do not forsake your mother's teaching.
They will be a garland to grace your head
and a chain to adorn your neck.

—Proverbs 1:8

We have tried to share with our children, grandchildren, and now our great-grandchildren a vital living faith in God that relates to the nitty-gritty needs of our lives. We have presented Christ to them, not just as a spirit, a concept, an idea, or a symbol, but as a person! One who walks by our side as our friend and daily companion.

From the time they were small, we have tried to build a sense of God's goodness into their lives. We taught them that:

- God is a good God.

- Everyone is somebody in God's eyes, and God is concerned about every part of our lives—no need is too big or too small to be included in His concern.

One of the first things our children learned was that God loves them. Even before they could talk, I found that I could plant seeds in their minds. I would point to a picture of Jesus on the wall and say, "That's Jesus, and He loves you."

It is never too early to start teaching your children that God loves them, completely and unconditionally—that they or you need never be afraid to come to Him. Jesus said, "Let the little children come to me, and do not hinder them, for the kingdom of God belongs to such as these" (Mark 10:14).[92]

make **your** day count

Look for ways that God shows His love for you and your children and share your insights with your kids. Lead them in a prayer of thanksgiving for God's goodness in their lives.

Developing Godly Desires

Gloria Copeland

Jesus said, "Look! I have been standing at the door, and I am constantly knocking. If anyone hears me calling him and opens the door I will come in and fellowship with him and he with me."
—Revelation 3:20 TLB

God wants us to go to church, to be loving toward everyone, and serve Him, but He wants us to do those things because we have a heartfelt desire. This only comes by spending time with God. The more we do, however, the more this desire grows.

It probably amazes some when they see thousands of people come to our conventions and spend an entire week— sometimes even vacation time—listening to the Word of God being taught. But these people have developed that desire by abiding in Jesus and spending time with Him.

Of course, there are some who hear a little about faith, find out that if they'll act on the Word it will bring blessing into their lives, and think, *Well, I'll try that.* So they listen to a message and then try to put what they've learned into action, without ever establishing a lifestyle of living in communion with God. It doesn't work.

It doesn't matter if you've been a believer and in the ministry for twenty-five years. If you stop communing and communicating with God on a daily basis, you'll begin to slip. That's because communion with God can't be stored up. It can't be learned and then put away. It has to be maintained continually if you want to have a fruitful life.[93]

make **your** day count

Time with God is an opportunity to get to know the best friend you will every have. Take advantage of time in the shower or car as time to talk with Him. Perhaps thinking about a particular Bible verse throughout the day fits your personality and lifestyle. Ask God to help you recognize what will work best for you.

Complementing One Another

Marilyn Hickey

The LORD God said, It is not good that the man should
be alone; I will make him an help meet for him.
—Genesis 2:18 KJV

There has been much misunderstanding regarding a
wife's relationship to her husband. Eve was to be a "help
meet" for Adam. A "help meet" is an alter ego, someone who
complements the husband. To *complement* means "to complete or bring to perfection, something added to complete a
whole." Rather than be a slave or a servant, the woman was
added to the man for the purpose of completion.

One time my husband really got after me about my
checkbook, and I said, "Well, don't you understand why the
Lord had me marry you? It's because He saw that I was
lacking in this area, and He gave me to you so that you could
help me!"

Marriage partners are to complement each other, not
compete with each other. If there is an area where you are
lacking and your spouse is a help, that's wonderful. Together
you make a complete, beautiful picture. When your relationship is complete, you complement each other. You are one,
and Jesus makes the two of you complete, for we are complete in Him.

God said, "I see that Adam needs a help meet, someone to meet his needs, and someone whose needs he can meet." The Bible tells us that God made all of His creation to be "very good." (Gen. 1:31.)[94]

make **your** day count

Think about ways in which you and your husband complete one another.

What strengths do each of you bring to the relationship?

Make a point to use one of your strengths to bless your husband today,

and thank God for the way your husband completes you.

Respond to Your Children's Questions

Pat Harrison

I call on you, O God, for you will answer me.
—Psalm 17:6

Kids ask lots of questions. You do not have to be ashamed to say to your adolescent child, "I'm not sure of the answer now, so I am going to pray to make sure I give you the right answer." What you should never say is "Well, I don't know, so don't worry about it." That is no answer at all—especially to a teenager.

After you tell your child, "Don't do this," and they ask why, do not allow yourself to say, "Because I said so." Whether or not your children like what you have to say, give them a real answer. If they do not get answers from you, they will go elsewhere to find them, and they may receive faulty or even dangerous information.

I have counseled teenagers whose parents told them, "You're not old enough to understand." If children are old enough to ask, they are old enough to understand. When your children come to you for answers, get your Bible out and look for what God says about their questions. Then express the answer in the simplest way you can. Teach them to look to the

Bible for their answers, so they do not ask someone else. They should trust you and the Bible for the truth.[95]

make **your** day count

Have your children asked you questions lately that perhaps you should have answered more fully? If so, provide them with the answers they need. Today, let your children know you have an "open door" policy and invite them to ask questions.

A Gift From the Kitchen

Beverage mixes make great gifts for just about anyone on your gift-giving list. Simply fill canning jars or any decorative containers with the mix. The dollar store is a great place to find inexpensive decorative jars for practically any holiday. Be sure to include the directions for preparing the drink by tying them on the lid with decorative ribbon or string.

The Internet is a great place to find recipes for different kinds of mixes, or use your own recipe. Here's one you might like to try.

> 2 cups instant lemon tea
> 3 ½ cups sugar
> 1 tsp. cinnamon
> 2 tsp. allspice
> 1 tsp. cloves

Mix together and store in an air-tight container. Use 3 teaspoons of the mix with 1 cup hot water.

Ziploc® Ice Cream[96]

This is a cute idea that can be done with a group of children.

½ cup milk (any kind, whole, 2%, or chocolate)
1 Tbsp. sugar
1/4 tsp. vanilla
Pint-size Ziploc freezer bags
Quart or larger Ziploc freezer bags
Ice
6 Tbsp. rock or regular salt

Add all ingredients to a pint-size Ziploc bag and zip shut.

Place that bag inside a larger, quart-size Ziploc bag.

Add ice to fill bag halfway plus salt (rock or regular).

Zip larger bag shut, and shake, turn, toss, and mix the bag. In about 5 to 10 minutes, you will have cold hands and yummy ice cream.

Note: does not work well to double the recipe.

Be sure to get all the salt off the small bag before opening it.

My Peace I Give You

Lindsay Roberts

Jesus said, "Peace I leave with you; my peace I give you.
I do not give to you as the world gives. Do not let
your hearts be troubled and do not be afraid."
—John 14:27

Right now, people everywhere are scared to death of what the future holds because of the events of September 11. The world is in chaos, and people are looking for a safety net. Many are facing circumstances never seen before and wondering where to turn for answers.

But we have to remember that when the twin towers in New York City came down, Jesus didn't fall off His throne. God didn't shake in His boots. He is still sovereign! And He's saying to us, "Call upon Me. Listen to Me. Don't worry. I am with you. Don't be afraid." His Word reassures us in John 14:27 that Jesus left us His peace. God is here to help us!

When the world situation looks dark as it did that horrendous day, how much brighter the light of our salvation shines! And yes, it's possible that things might get even darker, but God's Word tell us that we're not to be afraid, because when His praises fill us, we can receive His benefits and His strength!

When your mouth, your heart, and your spirit bless the Lord, you can be filled with the peace of God that surpasses all human understanding, no matter what is going on around you. (Phil. 4:7.) God wants to calm your fears and bring you peace and strength in times of crisis.[97]

make **your** day count

Jesus left you His peace, a peace not affected by what is going on in the world. Whenever you feel worried or afraid today, go to your heavenly Father, rest in His arms, and soak up His boundless peace.

Have You Read the Instructions?

Patricia Salem

Choose my instruction instead of silver,
knowledge rather than choice gold.
—Proverbs 8:10

I began having frequent headaches due to the abundant allergens in Oklahoma. To combat them, I began taking a couple of aspirin daily—often on an empty stomach. I had not considered the fact that as we get older, our bodies change and can react differently to medications than they did when we were younger.

One day something went terribly wrong. I started hemorrhaging and called Lindsay to rush me to the hospital, where I was diagnosed with a bleeding ulcer. The irony was that it could have been avoided, as my four-year-old great-grandson so brilliantly stated: "Mimi, do you think that maybe you should have read the instructions?"

Of course, he was right! And it's the same with our lives as believers. God doesn't want us to have to learn things the hard way. That's why He's given us the "instructions" in His Word—to benefit us so that we can know His will and be guided by His Spirit. If we are diligent to study His Word on a daily basis, many of the problems we might otherwise face can be avoided. And with the problems we can't avoid, we can draw upon the wisdom of God's Word. The next time you're faced with a problem, remember the simple wisdom of a child and read the instructions.[98]

make **your** day count

The book of Proverbs in the Bible is loaded with wise instructions for our daily lives. There are thirty-one chapters in Proverbs, which means there is a different chapter for each day of the month. Whatever today's date is, read the corresponding chapter and follow today's instructions.

Keeping the Shower Clean

Betsy Williams

To make cleaning a shower easier and to keep it clean longer, hang a squeegee (which you can purchase at a discount store) and a hand towel in your shower stall. After showering, squeegee the walls. Then use the hand towel to dry any water that has collected along the caulk. This will help to prevent mildew from forming. Finally, use the towel to dry all of the metal fixtures to prevent hard-water spots. This only takes a minute or two, but when it comes time to do a major cleaning, it'll be a snap.

Hawaiian Chicken[99]

4 to 6 skinless, boneless chicken breasts
¼ cup soy sauce (or liquid aminos)*
1 peeled, chopped kiwi
1 8-oz. can crushed pineapple
2 green onions, chopped
⅛ tsp. ground ginger
Dash of ground pepper

Rinse chicken.

Drain pineapple, reserving the liquid.

Place pineapple liquid and soy sauce in a large skillet. Bring to a boil over high heat.

Place chicken in mixture. Return to a boil.

Reduce heat, cover, and simmer approximately 10 minutes or until chicken is thoroughly cooked.

Meanwhile, place kiwi, pineapple, onion, ginger, and pepper in a small saucepan over medium to low heat until warm (approximately 3 minutes).

To serve, remove chicken from skillet and spoon fruit mixture over chicken.

Tip: Chicken can be cooked ahead of time and heated in the soy mixture.

*Available at health-food stores.

God Wants Us to Be Healthy!

Dee Simmons

Do you not know that your body is a temple
of the Holy Spirit, who is in you?
—1 Corinthians 6:19

We sometimes forget that our bodies are God's temple, and we would never purposefully neglect His temple. But when you hear the word *cancer*, you become ready and willing to do whatever is required to maintain good health.

Following my cancer surgery, my studies and travels led me to a different way of life, and without giving up one important thing, I changed the way I was living. I changed my dietary habits entirely for the better by eliminating most of the "bad" foods and adding fruits, vegetables, and whole grains in abundance. I began a serious nutrition and exercise program and became a student of preventive medicine.

With an improved diet and optimum nutrition, I know that I am really tending "my temple" and offering thanks to God through the practice of the very principles He set down in the Bible. Remember, "Whether you eat or drink or what- ever you do, do it all for the glory of God" (1 Cor. 10:31).

Today at sixty-three, I am enjoying the best health, the highest energy levels, and a joyous spiritual life. I have dis- covered that worship is not just attending church regularly, saying prayers, and participating in charitable endeavors. We can show worship by our choices—in our lifestyles and nutrition. What better way to give thanks for our health than to maintain it![100]

make **your** day count

Instead of taking something out of your life, what could you add to your life today that would be investment in your overall physical health?

Teaching Your Children About Their Bodies

Pat Harrison

Use every part of your body to give glory back to God.
—1 Corinthians 6:20 TLB

So many children feel condemned when they become teenagers because they start having thoughts about their own bodies or the bodies of others. If you have taught your children properly, they will know where those thoughts are coming from and what to do about them. And if they ever have a problem in this area, they will come to you for help.

Never allow your child to be ashamed of his or her body. God made the physical body. He put every part together, and every part has a specific purpose. Present it this way to your child, and your child will grow up understanding in a healthy way what the body is for.

One aspect of teaching your children about their bodies is training them in personal hygiene. For instance, so many girls do not know anything about the menstrual cycle because their mothers have never talked to them about it. The thought of it scares these adolescent girls because they do not understand that it is a normal part of growing up.

Some mothers think, *My daughter probably won't begin menstruating until she is twelve, so I'll wait until then to talk to her about it.* Don't wait! It is surprising how young some girls are when they begin their monthly cycles. If your daughter happens to be one of those girls, you don't want her to have to have that experience without the knowledge she needs to help her get through it.

If your children want to know about their bodies, take them to Genesis 1. Explain that God made Adam; then He saw that Adam needed a woman. You can go from there to explain the whole process that leads to the birth of a new life.[101]

make **your** day count

Initiate a discussion with your children about some aspect of their bodies, depending on their maturity level. If nothing else, point out what a miraculous creation their bodies are and that many of the functions necessary to sustain life are working continuously and accurately, without their even having to think about it.

Overcoming Temptation

Gloria Copeland

Through Christ Jesus the law of the Spirit of life
set me free from the law of sin and death.

—Romans 8:2

Constant fellowship with God will give you the power to become temperate and have self-control in every area of your life. It will enable you to conquer strongholds of sin that for years may have been conquering you!

Some expect to be free of such strongholds the moment they are born again. But, in most cases, acquiring that freedom takes place over time. That's because the new birth takes place in our spirits. It makes us new on the inside, but on the outside we have the same old bodies, usually with the same old habits.

We must strengthen our spirits so they can take precedence over our bodies and tell them what to do. Fellowshiping with God in prayer and His Word helps us do that. When we spend time meditating on God's Word, it works like spiritual food, strengthening the inner man, so we can rise up on the inside and take dominion over those fleshly sins and weaknesses that hinder us. It purifies us of ungodly thoughts, attitudes, and behaviors and keeps us abiding in Him.

Just as the power of the Holy Spirit and the fruit of the Spirit wither when you lose your communion with God, the power of sin withers when you maintain communion with Him. That is the principle of abiding in the vine. (John 15:4–5.)[102]

make **your** day count

Just as exercise strengthens your body, time in prayer and God's Word strengthens your spirit. Today, incorporate time with God into your schedule as you would time for a workout or walk around your neighborhood.

Share God's Presence

Evelyn Roberts

You must think constantly about these commandments I am giving you today. You must teach them to your children and talk about them when you are at home or out for a walk; at bedtime and the first thing in the morning.

—Deuteronomy 6:6–7 TLB

Family devotions were spontaneous in our household while our children were growing up. There was no set rule or rigid pattern. We tried to keep in mind that it was family worship, not parent worship. I feel that regimented devotions often become commonplace, and the children begin to think, *Oh, this is just one of the things that Mother and Dad do,* and it has no special meaning for them.

One effective thing we did when our children were little was to have a box of Bible promise cards at the breakfast table. Each card had one short verse on it. The children took turns picking a card and reading the verse out loud. Then we all talked about it for a minute.

We also found that when the children were big enough, they liked to take turns saying the blessing before each meal. In fact, if we missed one, they were sure to call it to our attention.

The *how* of conducting family devotions is not nearly as important as the *why.* When you gather as a family to center your hearts and minds on God, you are bringing your children into the presence of God Himself. You are helping them develop a greater understanding of God and a deeper love for Him.[103]

make **your** day count

Adopt this idea or perhaps keep a book of Bible promises in the car, so you can discuss a verse from time to time. Making a verse relevant to your children will help God's Word to take root in their hearts.

When You Have the Father, You Have It All

Lindsay Roberts

Bless the LORD, O my soul: and all that is
within me, bless his holy name. Bless the LORD,
O my soul, and forget not all his benefits.
—Psalm 103:1–2 KJV

People have asked me, "How can you be cheerful in times like these?"

I remind them that when you have the Father, you get all the properties and benefits of the Father: healing, health, salvation, miracles, redemption, peace—the whole shebang!

If my throat feels dry, the only way I know to get my throat wet is to take a drink of water. When I drink the water, I get all the properties of the water. If you get the water, you get the wet! When you get God, you get all of God!

If you knew that praising God would drill a hole into heaven, what would you be doing right now? *Praising and worshiping God!* You can't get the benefits if you are still holding on to fears and doubts and a bundle of bad attitudes. God is waiting for you to release all the junk that is filling your soul. He needs you to be empty, so He can forgive your sins, heal your diseases, redeem your life from destruction, and fill you with His loving-kindness, tender mercies, and peace.

Instead of worrying about your problems, begin to talk to the Father. Begin praising and thanking Him for His endless benefits. Fill your vessel—your soul—with the Lord, and reap His benefits![104]

make **your** day count

Begin releasing any of the "junk" that is filling your thoughts. In its place, fill your mind with thoughts of God's goodness and the many benefits available to His followers as in Psalm 103:1–5.

About the Author

Lindsay Roberts and her husband, Richard, were married in 1980. She began traveling with her husband, ministering throughout the world and supporting him in what the Lord has called him to do.

"After the birth of our son, Richard Oral," Lindsay says, "we were devastated when he lived only 36 hours. But God picked us up, dried our tears, and helped us try again." Out of that experience from pain to victory, Lindsay wrote *36 Hours with an Angel*—the story of how God sustained their faith after Richard Oral's death and blessed her and Richard with the miracle births of their three daughters: Jordan, Olivia, and Chloe.

Lindsay hosts *Make Your Day Count*, a daily television program full of ministry, cooking, creative tips, and lots of fun. With her husband, Richard, she also co-hosts the nightly television program *The Hour of Healing*.

Lindsay has co-authored several books, such as *A Cry for Miracles* and *Dear God, I Love to Eat, But I Sure Do Hate to Cook* cookbook. She has also written several children's books, including *ABC's of Faith for Children* and *God's Champions*.

Lindsay serves as editor of *Make Your Day Count*, a quarterly magazine aimed at today's woman; *Miracles Now*, a quarterly magazine for ministry partners; and *Your Daily Guide to Miracles*, a daily devotional book published semi-annually.

She is also a member of the Oral Roberts University Board of Regents.

"I am dedicated to God and willing to do whatever He calls me to do," Lindsay says. "I also stand in support of the call of God upon my husband. He and I are both grateful that God is using us for His glory."

Royalties from the sale of this book and others in the *Make Your Day Count* series will go towards the Make Your Day Count Scholarship Fund.

To contact Lindsay Roberts
or request a free issue of the
Make Your Day Count magazine,
please write to:

Lindsay Roberts
c/o Oral Roberts Ministries
Tulsa, Oklahoma 74171-0001
or
e-mail her at:
Lindsay@orm.cc

Please visit the *Make Your Day Count* Web site at
www.makeyourdaycount.com.

*Please include your prayer requests
and comments when you write.*

If you would like to have someone join in agreement with you in prayer as a point of contact, consider calling the Abundant Life Prayer Group at 918-495-7777. They are there to pray with you twenty-four hours a day, seven days a week.

About the Contributors

Deborah Butler is the first lady of Word of Faith International Christian Center in Southfield, MI; Word of Faith Christian Center in San Antonio, TX; and Faith Christian Center in Phoenix, AZ, where she serves in ministry with her husband, Bishop Keith A. Butler. She is a licensed and ordained minister, serving as the director of Women of Virtue fellowships and has been a Lindsay Roberts Women's Conference speaker. She and Bishop Butler have three children: Rev. Keith A. Butler II and his wife, Minister Tiffany Butler; Minister MiChelle Butler; and Minister Kristina Butler. To contact Deborah, call (248) 353-3476 or visit www.wordof-faith-icc.org.

Gloria Copeland is an author, teacher, and ordained minister alongside her husband, Kenneth Copeland. Together they've reached millions around the world with the message that God's Word works. Gloria has been a Lindsay Roberts Women's Conference speaker, and in 1986, she received an Honorary Doctorate of Humane Letters from Oral Roberts University. In 1994, she was voted Christian Woman of the Year. You may contact Gloria by calling (800) 600-7395 or visiting www.kcm.org.

Marty Copeland is a certified personal trainer, fitness instructor, and nutritional guidance counselor. She is a wife and mother of three children. For more information on **weight loss** and **fitness products** you may contact Marty at **www.martycopeland.com** or by calling (800) 600-7395.

Sharon Daugherty co-pastors alongside her husband, Pastor Billy Joe Daugherty at Victory Christian Center in Tulsa, Oklahoma. In 1976, Sharon earned a bachelor's degree in Music Education from Oral Roberts University. She is an anointed worship leader, psalmist, author, and teacher and has been a Lindsay Roberts Women's Conference speaker. The Daughertys are involved in outreaches through TV, radio, literature, and crusades in the United States and in other nations. She and her husband have four children. To contact Sharon, call (918) 491-7700 or visit www.victorytulsa.org.

Taffi L. Dollar and her husband, Dr. Creflo A. Dollar Jr., pastor World Changers Church in College Park, Georgia, where she serves as the vice president of the ministry, president and CEO of Arrow records, and overseer of the Women's Fellowship. Taffi is an author and teacher and has been a Lindsay Roberts Women's Conference speaker. Taffi earned a bachelor's degree in Mental Health and Human Services from Georgia State University. To contact Taffi, visit www.worldchangers.org or call (770) 210-5850.

Shelley Fenimore has appeared on *Make Your Day Count* as a guest and as a co-host several times. She and her husband, Rick, a graduate of Oral Roberts University, reside in Tulsa, Oklahoma, with their three children. They are longtime partners with Oral Roberts Ministries.

Pat Harrison is known as a woman who loves the Holy Spirit. She is a successful author, speaker, and leader whose ministry encourages people to develop a personal walk with God and to get to know the person of the Holy Spirit. Pat is a member of the Oral Roberts University Board of Regents and has been a Lindsay Roberts Women's Conference speaker. Pat and her late husband, Buddy, founded Faith Christian Fellowship International in Tulsa, Oklahoma. The ministry is affiliated with over three thousand churches worldwide. To contact Pat, call (918) 492-5800 or visit www.fcf.org.

Marilyn Hickey's mission is to "cover the earth with the Word," which has been effectively accomplished through worldwide speaking, writing, television, and the establishment of a fully accredited two-year Bible college. In 1986, Marilyn received an Honorary Doctorate of Divinity from Oral Roberts University. She is Chairman of the Board of Regents at Oral Roberts University, a member of the International Charismatic Bible Ministries Board of Trustees, and has been a Lindsay Roberts Women's Conference speaker. Marilyn is married to Wallace Hickey, pastor of Orchard Road Christian Center in Greenwood Village, Colorado. They have two grown children. You may contact Marilyn by calling (303) 770-0400 or visiting www.mhmin.org.

Kellie Copeland Kutz is a speaker, author, musician, wife, and mother of four. She directs the development of all Kenneth Copeland Ministries' children's product and is the contributing editor for *Shout! The Voice of Victory for Kids*, a monthly children's magazine. She is best known as Commander Kellie—the fearless, faith-filled adventurer in the *Commander Kellie and the SuperKids*^{SM} videos, audio series, and novels. To contact Kellie, visit www.kcm.org or call (800) 600-7395.

Dodie Osteen, wife of the late Pastor John Osteen, has a mighty ministry of love and compassion. Healed of cancer by standing on God's Word, she has inspired hope and faith in countless numbers of people. In 1991, Dodie received an Honorary Doctorate of Humane Letters from Oral Roberts University. She is also a registered nurse. To contact Dodie, visit www.lakewood.cc or call (713) 635-4154.

Evelyn Roberts, wife of Evangelist Oral Roberts, has been by his side in the ministry for over fifty years. Mrs. Roberts is Lindsay Roberts' mother-in-law. She is the author of several books and is a Lifetime Spiritual Regent on the Oral Roberts University Board of Regents. She is also a member of the International Charismatic Bible Ministries Board of Trustees and has been a speaker at the Lindsay Roberts Women's Conferences. Mrs. Roberts attended Northeastern State University in Oklahoma and Texas College of Arts and Industries in Kingville, Texas. She taught school for three years before marrying Oral. They are the parents of four children; thirteen grandchildren, one of whom is in heaven; and thirteen great-grandchildren. For more information, visit www.orm.cc.

Patricia Salem has been a partner with Oral Roberts Ministries since the 1950s, when she was miraculously healed of cancer through reading one of Oral Roberts' books. She moved to Tulsa in the eighties, after her daughter, Lindsay, entered the Oral Roberts University School of Law. In 2003, Patricia received an Honorary Doctorate of Divinity from Oral Roberts University, and she can be seen with Lindsay daily on the *Make Your Day Count* television broadcast. For more information, visit www.orm.cc.

Dee Simmons is a member of the Oral Roberts University Board of Regents and has been a Lindsay Roberts Women's Conference speaker. She is founder and chairman of her own nutrition company, Ultimate Living International, a nutritional product manufacturer and distributor. Her daily nutritional program, *Health Views*, is seen across the nation. Dee has been the national spokesperson for Making Memories Breast Cancer Foundation since 1999. To contact Dee, call (214) 220-1240 or visit www.ultimateliving.com.

Brenda Timberlake-White graduated with honors from Fayetteville State University in Fayetteville, North Carolina, in 1971 and Bread from Heaven Bible Institute in 1981. She and her husband, the late Bishop Mack Timberlake, served as the senior pastors of Christian Faith Center in Creedmoor, North Carolina. Following the passing of her husband, Brenda accepted the mantle to serve as senior pastor. She is a member of the International Charismatic Bible Ministries Board of Trustees and has been a Lindsay Roberts Women's Conference speaker. She is a governor on the Board of Governors for the National Center for Faith-based Initiatives and is the proud mother of four daughters and three sons. To contact Brenda, call (919) 528-1581 or visit www.timberlakeministries.com.

Betsy Williams is a freelance editor/writer, specializing in inspirational books. Her work has appeared in publications from a variety of publishers in the Christian bookselling industry, including several major publishers. Originally from Huntsville, Alabama, she is a 1983 graduate of Rhema Bible Training Center in Tulsa, Oklahoma, where she and her family currently reside. Betsy and her husband, Jim, are the proud parents of two active boys. She may be contacted at williams.services.inc@cox.net.

Julie Wilson is a native of Pittsburgh, Pennsylvania. She and her husband, Jim, are both graduates of Oral Roberts University and are Certified Public Accountants in Tulsa, Oklahoma. She is a regional representative with Stonecroft Ministries and often speaks to Christian Women's Clubs throughout the country. She and Jim have three sons.

Endnotes

1   Lindsay Roberts, *Make Your Day Count* magazine (Tulsa, OK: Oral Roberts Evangelistic Association, April–June 2003) p. 4.
2   Evelyn Roberts, *Make Your Day Count* magazine (April–June 2001) p. 6.
3   Patricia Salem, *Make Your Day Count* magazine (April–June 2003) pp. 14–15.
4   <AngieCooks@tripod.net> 3237 E. Sunshine, Suite A 194, Springfield, MO 65804; <http://members.tripod.com/AngieCooks/kids/backtoschool.html> (accessed November 2003).
5   Patricia Salem, *Richard & Lindsay Roberts Family Cookbook* (Tulsa, OK: Oral Roberts Evangelistic Association, 1990), p. 198.
6   Kellie Copeland Kutz, "Make Sure Your Children Are Protected" (Fort Worth, TX: Kenneth Copeland Ministries, <www.kcm.org> 2003). *Protecting Your Family in Dangerous Times* (Tulsa, OK: Harrison House Publishers, 2002) pp. 1–3.
7   Marty Copeland, "One Step at a Time…How to Win at Weight Loss and Fitness" (Ft. Worth, TX: Kenneth Copeland Ministries) <http://kcm.org/studycenter/articles/health_healing/how_to_win_at_weight_loss.html> (accessed 11/03).
8   Marilyn Hickey, *The Spirit-Filled Mother's Guide to Total Victory* (Tulsa, OK: Harrison House Publishers, 1994) pp. 79–80.
9   Taffi L. Dollar, *Changing Your World* magazine, "Developing Your Children's Future" (College Park, GA: Creflo Dollar Ministries, Nov. 2002) <www.creflodollarministries.org/pdf/nov02.pdf> (accessed Sept. 2003).
10 Lindsay Roberts, *Make Your Day Count* magazine (Oct.–Dec. 2001) p. 34.
11 Mack and Brenda Timberlake, *Heaven on Earth in Your Marriage* (Tulsa, OK: Harrison House Publishers, 1993) pp. 7–13.
12 Pat Harrison, *The Great Balancing Act* (Tulsa, OK: Harrison House Publishers, 2002), pp. 3–6.
13 Naturalife Health Ltd., Co. Wicklow, Ireland, <http://www.naturalife.ie/hdocs/shop_udo.html> (accessed Oct. 2003).
14 Excerpt from *The Body Ecology Diet* by Donna Gates, <http://www.holisticmed.com/sweet/stv-cook.txt> (accessed Oct. 2003).
15 Pat Harrison, *Richard & Lindsay Roberts Family Cookbook*, p. 166.
16 Marilyn Hickey, *God's Covenant for Your Family* (Tulsa, OK: Harrison House Publishers, 1982) pp. 106–107.
17 Marty Copeland, "One Step at a Time…How to Win at Weight Loss and Fitness (Ft. Worth, TX: Kenneth Copeland Ministries) <http://kcm.org/studycenter/articles/health_healing/how_to_win_at_weight_loss.html> (accessed 11/03).
18 Lindsay Roberts, *36 Hours with an Angel* (Tulsa, OK: Oral Roberts Evangelistic Association, Inc., 1990) pp. 121–122, 126.
19 Evelyn Roberts, *Make Your Day Count* magazine (July–Sept. 2002) pp. 30–31.
20 "Helpful Tips and Hints," <http://www.baycooking.com/kitchen_tips.htm> (accessed Oct. 2003).
21 Evelyn Roberts, *Richard & Lindsay Roberts Family Cookbook*, p. 71.
22 Taffi L. Dollar, "So, Your Kids Want to Date?" *Changing Your World Magazine* (Sept. 2003) p. 12.
23 Kellie Copeland Kutz, "Make Sure Your Children Are Protected," <http://kcm.org/studycenter/articles/protection/your_childs_protection.html> (accessed Sept. 2003); *Protecting Your Family in Dangerous Times* (Tulsa, OK: Harrison House Publishers, 2002) pp. 11–18.
24 Julie Wilson, *Make Your Day Count* broadcast #1834 (Tulsa, OK: Oral Roberts Evangelistic Association) aired March 20, 2003.
25 Pat Harrison, *The Great Balancing Act*, pp. 135, 137–139.
26 Marilyn Hickey, *God's Covenant for Your Family*, pp. 26–27, 29.
27 Evelyn Roberts, *Make Your Day Count* magazine (April–June 2001), pp. 6–7.
28 Taffi L. Dollar, "So, Your Kids Want to Date?" *Changing Your World Magazine* (Sept. 2003) p. 13.
29 Kellie Copeland Kutz, "Make Sure Your Children Are Protected" <http://kcm.org/studycenter/articles/protection/your_childs_protection.html> (accessed Sept. 2003); *Protecting Your Family in Dangerous Times* (Tulsa, OK: Harrison House Publishers, 2002) pp. 4–8.

[30] Lindsay Roberts, *Make Your Day Count* magazine (Jan.–March 2003) pp. 7–8.

[31] About, Inc., "Lighter: Healthy Substitutions for Baking"; <http://www.homecooking.about.com/gi/dynamic/offsite.htm?site=http://www.foodwine.com/food/egg/egg0196/lightsub.html> (accessed Oct. 2003).

[32] Lindsay Roberts, *Richard & Lindsay Roberts Family Cookbook*, p. 10.

[33] Marty Copeland, "The Body/Finance Connection" (Ft. Worth, TX: Kenneth Copeland Ministries 2003) <http://www.kcm.org/studycenter/articles/health_healing/more_than_resolution.html> (accessed Nov. 2003).

[34] Pat Harrison, *The Great Balancing Act*, pp. 140–143.

[35] Taffi L. Dollar, *Changing Your World Magazine*, "Loving the Woman in the Mirror" (College Park, GA: Creflo Dollar Ministries, March 2002) pp. 5–6.

[36] Evelyn Roberts, *How to Raise Your Children in God's Love* (Tulsa, OK: Oral Roberts Evangelistic Association, 1982) pp. 20–21.

[37] Marilyn Hickey, *Breaking Generational Curses* (Tulsa, OK: Harrison House Publishers, 2000) pp. 7–8.

[38] Kelli Copeland Kutz, "Make Sure Your Children Are Protected," <www.kcm.org> (accessed Sept. 2003); *Protecting Your Family in Dangerous Times* (Tulsa, OK: Harrison House Publishers, 2002) pp. 6–8.

[39] Lindsay Roberts, *Make Your Day Count* magazine (April–June 2001) pp. 9–12.

[40] Lindsay Roberts, *Richard & Lindsay Roberts Family Cookbook*, p. 113.

[41] Evelyn Roberts, *How to Raise Your Children in God's Love*, pp. 7–8.

[42] Pat Harrison, *The Great Balancing Act*, pp. 151–154.

[43] Taffi L. Dollar, *Changing Your World Magazine*, (Sept. 2003) p. 14.

[44] Sharon Daugherty, *The Spirit-Filled Mother's Guide to Total Victory* (Tulsa, OK: Harrison House Publishers, 1994) pp. 131–36.

[45] Sharon Daugherty, *Richard & Lindsay Roberts Family Cookbook*, p. 10.

[46] Deborah Butler, *Make Your Day Count* magazine (May–June 2001) pp. 28–29.

[47] Kellie Copeland Kutz, "Make Sure Your Children Are Protected," <www.kcm.org> (accessed Sept. 2003); *Protecting Your Family in Dangerous Times* (Tulsa, OK: Harrison House Publishers, 2002) pp. 9–10.

[48] Gloria Copeland, "A Word About Your Children" (Ft. Worth, TX: Kenneth Copeland Ministries) <http://kcm.org/studycenter/articles/relationships/word_about_your_children.html> (accessed Nov. 2003).

[49] Gloria Copeland, "When God Says 'Pssst!'" (Ft. Worth, TX: Kenneth Copeland Ministries) <http://kcm.org/studycenter/articles/protection/whengodsayspssst.html> (accessed Nov. 2003).

[50] Gloria Copeland, *Richard & Lindsay Roberts Family Cookbook*, p. 51.

[51] Evelyn Roberts, *Miracles Now* (April—June 2003) p. 6.

[52] Marilyn Hickey, *Breaking Generational Curses*, pp. 8–9.

[53] A. E. Winship.

[54] Ibid.

[55] Lindsay Roberts, *A Cry for Miracles* (Tulsa, OK: Lindsay Roberts, 1996) pp. 124–126.

[56] Shelley Fenimore, *Hour of Healing* broadcast #1423 (Tulsa, OK: Oral Roberts Evangelistic Association) aired March 3, 2003.

[57] Gloria Copeland, *Go with the Flow* (Tulsa, OK: Harrison House Publishers, 2001) pp. 5–9.

[58] Dee Simmons, *Make Your Day Count* magazine (April–June 2001) pp. 13–14.

[59] Dee Simmons, tips and recipe from *Make Your Day Count* broadcast.

[60] Lindsay Roberts, *StressLess Living* (Tulsa, OK: Harrison House Publishers, 2003) pp. 4–7.

[61] Taffi L. Dollar, *Changing Your World* magazine, "Good Cop, Bad Cop: Disciplining Children," (College Park: GA, Creflo Dollar Ministries, June 2002) pp. 12–13.

[62] Mack and Brenda Timberlake, *Heaven on Earth in Your Marriage*, pp. 19–20.

[63] Evelyn Roberts, *Richard & Lindsay Roberts Family Cookbook*, p. 187.

[64] Lindsay Roberts, *A Cry for Miracles*, pp. 151–156.

[65] Marilyn Hickey, "The Most Important Gift You Can Give Your Children," (P.O. Box 17340, Denver, CO 80217) <http://www.mhmin.org/MHarticles/mhgift.htm> (accessed Nov. 2003).

⁶⁶ Dodie Osteen, *Healed of Cancer* (Houston, TX: John Osteen, 1986) pp. 5, 14, 20–21, 24–25, 43.

⁶⁷ Dodie Osteen, *More Than a Cookbook Cookbook*, p. 152.

⁶⁸ Lindsay Roberts, *StressLess Living*, pp. 13–14.

⁶⁹ Patricia Salem, *Make Your Day Count* magazine (Oct.–Dec. 2001) pp. 10–11.

⁷⁰ Gloria Copeland, *To Know Him* (Tulsa, OK: Harrison House Publishers, 2003) pp. 1–2.

⁷¹ Evelyn Roberts, *How to Raise Your Children in God's Love*, pp. 8–9.

⁷² Lindsay Roberts, *Dear God, I Love to Eat…But I Sure Do Hate to Cook!* (Tulsa, OK: Lindsay Roberts, 2001) p. 93.

⁷³ Taffi L. Dollar, *Changing Your World* magazine, "Good Cop, Bad Cop: Disciplining Children," (College Park: GA, Creflo Dollar Ministries, June 2002) p. 13.

⁷⁴ Marilyn Hickey, "The Most Important Gift You Can Give Your Children"; <http://www.mhmin.org/MHarticles/mhgift.htm>. (accessed Nov. 2003).

⁷⁵ Dee Simmons, *Surviving Cancer*, (Tulsa, OK: Harrison House Publishers, 2001) pp. 157, 169.

⁷⁶ Dee Simmons, *Make Your Day Count* magazine (Oct.–Dec. 2002) p. 25.

⁷⁷ *Dear God, I Love to Eat…But I Sure Hate to Cook!* p. 20.

⁷⁸ Gloria Copeland, "When God Says 'Pssst!'" (Ft.Worth, TX: Kenneth Copeland Ministries) <http://kcm.org/studycenter/articles/protection/whengodsayspssst.html> (accessed Nov. 2003).

⁷⁹ Lindsay Roberts, *StressLess Living: Release the Pressures of Life and Start Enjoying Every Day* (Tulsa, OK: Harrison House Publishers, 2003) pp. 12–13.

⁸⁰ Marilyn Hickey, "The Most Important Gift You Can Give Your Children," <http://www.mhmin.org/MHarticles/mhgift.htm> (accessed Nov. 2003).

⁸¹ Pat Harrison, *The Great Balancing Act*, pp. 173–174.

⁸² Taffi L. Dollar, "Confessions for Successful Parenting," *Changing Your World Magazine* (Sept. 2003) p. 9.

⁸³ Patricia Salem, *Make Your Day Count* magazine (July–Aug. 2001) p. 30.

⁸⁴ Lindsay Roberts, *Make Your Day Count* magazine (July–Sept. 2001) p. 16.

⁸⁵ Herbert G. Lingren, "Put Laughter and Humor in Your Life"; University of Nebraska Cooperative Extension, Institute of Agriculture and Natural Resources, <http://www.ianr.unl.edu/pubs/family/nf389.htm> (accessed Nov. 2003).

⁸⁶ *Make Your Day Count* magazine (July–Sept. 2001) p. 16.

⁸⁷ Evelyn Roberts, *How to Raise Your Children in God's Love*, pp. 14–15.

⁸⁸ Marty Copeland, "More Than a New Year's Resolution" (Ft. Worth, TX: Kenneth Copeland Ministries) <http://www.kcm.org/studycenter/articles/health_healing/more_than_resolution.html> (accessed Nov. 2003).

⁸⁹ Marilyn Hickey, "The Most Important Gift You Can Give Your Children," <http://www.mhmin.org/MHarticles/mhgift.htm> (accessed Nov. 2003).

⁹⁰ Lindsay Roberts, *A Cry for Miracles*, pp. 123–124.

⁹¹ Taffi L. Dollar, "Deprogramming Your Kids," *Changing Your World Magazine* (Oct. 2003) p. 14.

⁹² Pat Harrison, *The Great Balancing Act*, pp. 174–177.

⁹³ Lindsay Roberts, *Make Your Day Count* (Jan.–March 2002) pp. 6–7.

⁹⁴ Eric W. Alderton, copyright © 1996, <http://www.ddc.com/cheferic/tips.htm> (accessed Nov. 2003).

⁹⁵ Evelyn Roberts, *How to Raise Your Children in God's Love*, pp. 9–10.

⁹⁶ Gloria Copeland, *To Know Him*, pp. 25–27.

⁹⁷ Marilyn Hickey, *God's Covenant for Your Family*, pp. 36–37.

⁹⁸ Pat Harrison, *The Great Balancing Act*, pp. 174–176.

⁹⁹ Dori Byron, <http://www.skl.com/~guidezon/jbice.htm> (accessed Nov. 2003).

¹⁰⁰ Lindsay Roberts, *Make Your Day Count* magazine (Jan.–March 2002) pp. 7–8.

¹⁰¹ Patricia Salem, *Make Your Day Count* magazine (Jan.–March 2002) p. 26.

¹⁰² *Make Your Day Count* magazine (Jan.–March 2002) p. 17.

¹⁰³ Dee Simmons, *Make Your Day Count* magazine (Jan.–March 2002) p. 21.

¹⁰⁴ Pat Harrison, *The Great Balancing Act*, pp. 171–172.

¹⁰⁵ Gloria Copeland, *To Know Him*, pp. 35–36.

¹⁰⁶ Evelyn Roberts, *How to Raise Your Children in God's Love*, pp. 18–19.

¹⁰⁷ Lindsay Roberts, *Make Your Day Count* magazine (Jan.–March 2002) p. 8.

Prayer of Salvation

God loves you—no matter who you are, no matter what your past. God loves you so much that He gave His one and only begotten Son for you. The Bible tells us that "whoever believes in him shall not perish but have eternal life" (John 3:16). Jesus laid down His life and rose again so that we could spend eternity with Him in heaven and experience His absolute best on earth. If you would like to receive Jesus into your life, say the following prayer out loud and mean it from your heart:

> *Heavenly Father, I come to You, admitting that I am a sinner. Right now, I choose to turn away from sin, and I ask You to cleanse me of all unrighteousness. I believe that Your Son, Jesus, died on the cross to take away my sins. I also believe that He rose again from the dead so that I might be forgiven of my sins and made righteous through faith in Him. I call upon the name of Jesus Christ to be the Savior and Lord of my life. Jesus, I choose to follow You and ask that You fill me with the power of the Holy Spirit. I declare that right now I am a child of God. I am free from sin and full of the righteousness of God. I am saved in Jesus' name. Amen.*

If you prayed this prayer to receive Jesus Christ as your Lord and Savior for the first time, please contact us on the Web at **www.harrisonhouse.com** to receive a free book.

Or you may write to us at

Harrison House
P.O. Box 35035
Tulsa, Oklahoma 74153

Other Books in the
Make Your Day Count Devotional Series

Make Your Day Count Devotional for Teachers
Make Your Day Count Devotional for Teens
Make Your Day Count Devotional for Women

Additional copies of this book
are available from your local bookstore.

If this book has been a blessing to you
or if you would like to see more of the
Harrison House product line,
please visit us on our Web site at
www.harrisonhouse.com.

HARRISON HOUSE
Tulsa, Oklahoma 74153

The Harrison House Vision

Proclaiming the truth and the power

Of the Gospel of Jesus Christ

With excellence;

Challenging Christians to

Live victoriously,

Grow spiritually,

Know God intimately.